COOKING WITH
Bon Appétit

COOKING WITH

Bon Appétit

Gifts from the Kitchen

THE KNAPP PRESS
Publishers
Los Angeles

Copyright © 1987 by Knapp Communications Corporation

Published by The Knapp Press
5900 Wilshire Boulevard, Los Angeles, California 90036

Library of Congress Cataloging in Publication Data

Main entry under title:

Gifts from the kitchen.

  (Cooking with Bon appétit)
  Includes index.
  1. Cookery. 2. Canning and preserving. 3. Gifts.
  I. Bon appétit. II. Series.
TX652.G538 1987   641.5   86-27191
ISBN 0-89535-179-X

On the cover: *Clockwise from right: Creamy Caramels, English Butter Toffee, Rocky Road. Photo by Brian Leatart*

Printed and bound in the United States of America

10 9 8 7 6 5 4 3 2 1

❦ Contents

Foreword . . . . *vii*

1 Spreads and Nuts *1*

2 Pâtés, Sausages
and Meat Pies *7*

3 Sauces, Salad Dressings
and Seasonings *17*
    Savory Sauces 18
    Sweet Sauces 22
    Flavored Oils, Vinegars and Mustards 26
    Seasonings 34

4 Pickles, Relishes
and Chutneys *37*

5 Jams and Preserves *51*

6 Breads, Cakes
and Cookies *63*
    Crackers and Breads 64
    Cakes and Cookies 82

7 Candy 99

Index 115

❧ *Foreword*

Giving a gift of food has long been a tradition throughout the world. Whatever the occasion, it has always been a gesture of respect and good wishes to enter a home with something delicious to eat—perhaps a pot of soup or a tray of fragrant, home-baked bread, something representing prosperity or the sharing of sustenance. In this age of high technology and culinary sophistication, a gift of homemade food is more than ever a warm, personal touch that is much appreciated, bringing pleasure to both the giver and the recipient.

The opportunities for presenting gifts from the kitchen are many. Some are traditional, such as holiday celebrations, birthdays or anniversaries. And some are more impromptu, such as a visit to a new mother who may not have the time to prepare a meal, or to a music teacher deserving of special thanks.

The kinds of food that can be given vary from a plate of cookies or a jar of homemade jam to an elegant pâté or a beautifully decorated tin of chocolates. Gifts of food should be portable, should keep well, and should be appropriate for the season. In the summer, keep it light and simple, like a sweet fruit sauce to spoon over ice cream or a picnic basket of mustards and cheese. In the winter, more substantial items such as rich fruitcakes or breads are always welcome.

Some of the recipes in this volume, such as the Old-Fashioned Gingerbread House (page 92) or The Four Seasons Fruitcake (page 91), require a little time to prepare. But there are many that can be done almost at the last minute, such as Spiked Pineapple Dessert Sauce (page 24), English Pub Mustard (page 34) and Easy Apricot Cake (page 83). Of course, some of our favorite gifts are those wonderful things that can be made days or even weeks ahead of time and taken from the pantry shelf to be festively wrapped and packaged—like Rosemary Vinegar (page 27) and Five-Fruit Marmalade (page 54). Many of these foods are so good, and the recipes so easy, you'll want to make them for yourself.

Because half the fun in giving these is the presentation, pay particular attention to the packaging. Begin collecting old-fashioned tins, pretty baskets and jars, and colorful trinkets and gift tags to tie on top. Combine foods—and they don't all have to be homemade—to make creative gifts. If you're in a hurry, whip up a special flavored mustard and put it in a ceramic crock alongside a spicy sausage from the delicatessen and a crisp loaf of French bread from the bakery, all wrapped up in a picnic basket complete with tablecoth and napkins. Above all, use your imagination: The recipes in this book are just a start, good ideas that will inspire you to put together your own great gifts from the kitchen.

1 ❦ Spreads and Nuts

Tasty spreads and flavored nuts are always a popular hostess or party gift. Whether the gathering is casual or formal, a tray of homemade cheese spread and crackers is sure to be welcome, and spiced nuts are something that everyone appreciates receiving—they're a great snack to keep on hand throughout the year.

One of the best things about the recipes in this chapter is that most of them can be made a day or more ahead. Mix up a crock of Viennese Liptauer (page 2) or Alsatian Cheese Spread (page 2) the day before you need it. Or, on a quiet afternoon, prepare a big batch of Spiced Pecans (page 3) or Coconut Granola (page 6) and put it in decorative jars to be given away during the holiday season.

But don't just save these for November or December. For that extra-special summer party, a variety of spiced nuts packed in a basket with an assortment of imported beers makes a great gift. And for an informal gathering any time of year, bring along a big bowl of freshly made Cheese-Garlic Popcorn (page 5)—it's sure to be a hit.

Alsatian Cheese Spread

Like the Liptauer that follows, this makes a lovely gift when presented in a pretty crock and accompanied by homemade crackers or breadsticks.

Makes about 1 cup

1 cup small curd cottage cheese
1 large garlic clove
1/4 teaspoon salt
3 tablespoons whipping cream

1 tablespoon chopped fresh parsley
Freshly ground white pepper

Press cottage cheese through strainer into medium bowl. Crush garlic clove with salt and add to cheese. Mix in remaining ingredients. Cover and refrigerate at least 1 hour or overnight. Serve at room temperature.

Viennese Liptauer

Makes 1 1/2 cups

1 cup cream cheese, room temperature
1/2 cup (1 stick) butter, room temperature
3 tablespoons sour cream
2 anchovy fillets
1 teaspoon capers, drained

1 tablespoon finely chopped onion
1 tablespoon Dijon mustard
1 1/2 teaspoons paprika
1 teaspoon caraway seed
1/2 teaspoon salt

Blend cheese, butter and sour cream in medium bowl. Mash anchovies and capers in small bowl. Mix into cheese. Stir in remaining ingredients. Transfer to serving bowl or mound on plate. Cover and refrigerate at least 1 hour or overnight. Serve cheese spread at room temperature.

Cumin Cheese Spread

Makes about 1 1/4 cups

1 teaspoon cumin seed
6 ounces soft goat cheese
6 ounces Monterey Jack cheese, cut into 1-inch cubes

1/4 cup (1/2 stick) unsalted butter, room temperature

Cook cumin seed in heavy small skillet over medium-high heat until fragrant but not brown, stirring occasionally, about 3 minutes. Remove from heat.

Mix together both cheeses, butter and cumin in processor until completely smooth, about 2 minutes, stopping as necessary to scrape down sides of work bowl. (*Can be prepared 1 week ahead and chilled.*) Serve at room temperature.

Anchoiade

Serve this tapénade as a first course with toasted French bread rounds, raw fennel, crisp-tender green beans, hard-cooked eggs and red peppers.

4 to 6 servings

4 2-ounce cans anchovies with capers
2 garlic cloves
1 bunch fresh basil leaves (1/3 to 1/2 cup)
2 tablespoons white wine vinegar
1 tablespoon Lime Mustard (page 31)

1/2 teaspoon thyme
1/4 cup plus 2 tablespoons olive oil
1/4 cup whipping cream

Rinse anchovies and drain well. Transfer to processor. Add garlic cloves and capers and blend well. Add basil, vinegar, mustard and thyme and blend until smooth and creamy. With machine running, add olive oil through feed tube in slow steady stream and blend until mixture is consistency of mayonnaise. Add whipping cream and mix well. Transfer to jar with tight-fitting lid. Refrigerate.

Spiced Pecans

Makes 4 cups

7 tablespoons unsalted butter
3 tablespoons chili powder
1¹/₂ teaspoons salt

³/₄ teaspoon cayenne pepper
¹/₂ teaspoon cinnamon
1 pound shelled whole pecans

Preheat oven to 350°F. Melt butter in heavy medium skillet over low heat. Stir in seasonings, then pecans to coat thoroughly with butter. Transfer pecans to baking sheet using slotted spoon. Bake until toasted, about 20 minutes. Drain on paper towels. Cool completely. Store in airtight jars.

Peppery Indian Cashew Nuts (Bhone Kaaju)

8 servings

1 pound raw cashews
2 teaspoons ground cumin
³/₄ teaspoon coarse kosher salt or to taste
¹/₂ teaspoon cayenne pepper
¹/₂ teaspoon freshly ground black pepper

¹/₄ teaspoon ground fennel seeds
Peanut oil or corn oil for deep frying

Rinse cashews under cold water. Pat dry with kitchen towel. Mix cumin, salt, cayenne pepper, black pepper and fennel in small bowl. Pour oil into heavy large skillet to depth of 1 inch. Heat to 325°F. Add cashews. Stir until light brown, about 5 minutes. Transfer to shallow dish using slotted spoon. Immediately toss with spices. Cool completely. (*Can be stored in airtight container at room temperature up to 2 weeks.*)

Chili Roasted Peanuts

Makes about 6 cups

2 tablespoons vegetable oil
4 garlic cloves, minced
1 tablespoon dried red pepper flakes

2 pounds salted peanuts
1 teaspoon chili powder

Preheat oven to 350°F. Heat oil in heavy large skillet over medium heat. Add garlic and pepper flakes and cook 1 minute. Add peanuts and stir to combine. Transfer peanuts to baking sheet. Bake until slightly browned, about 10 minutes. Sprinkle with chili powder and toss to combine. Cool completely. Cover and store in airtight container at least 8 hours.

Honeyed Walnuts

Makes 3 cups

1¹/₂ cups sugar
¹/₂ cup water
¹/₄ cup honey

3 cups walnuts
¹/₂ teaspoon vanilla

Cook sugar, water and honey in heavy medium saucepan over low heat until sugar dissolves, swirling pan occasionally. Increase heat and boil until candy thermometer registers 240°F (soft-ball stage). Remove from heat. Add walnuts and vanilla and stir until syrup is thick and cream-colored, about 5 minutes. Turn mixture out onto marble slab or sheet of lightly oiled waxed paper. Separate walnuts using 2 forks. Cool completely. Store in airtight container. (*Can be prepared 2 weeks ahead.*)

Glazed Pecans

Makes 1 pound

¹/₄ cup (¹/₂ stick) unsalted butter
¹/₄ cup light corn syrup
2 tablespoons water

1 teaspoon salt
1 pound pecan halves

Preheat oven to 250°F. Line baking sheet with foil. Combine butter, corn syrup, water and salt in heavy 1-quart saucepan and bring to boil. Stir in pecans, mixing to coat well. Spread evenly on baking sheet and bake 1 hour, stirring about every 10 minutes. Cool completely. Store in airtight container.

Glazed Spiced Nuts

Makes 1 pound

¹/₃ cup sugar
¹/₄ cup (¹/₂ stick) unsalted butter
¹/₄ cup fresh orange juice
1¹/₂ teaspoons salt
1¹/₄ teaspoons cinnamon
¹/₄ teaspoon cayenne pepper

¹/₄ teaspoon ground mace
1 pound unsalted mixed nuts (such as pecans, macadamias, peanuts, walnuts and unblanched almonds)

Position rack in center of oven and preheat to 250°F. Line jelly roll pan with foil. Cook sugar, butter, orange juice, salt, cinnamon, cayenne and mace in heavy large skillet over low heat until butter melts and sugar dissolves. Increase heat to medium. Add nuts and toss until coated. Spread in single layer on prepared pan. Bake 1 hour, stirring every 15 minutes.

Transfer nuts to large sheet of foil. Separate with fork or toothpick. Cool completely. Store in airtight container up to 5 days. (*Can be frozen 1 month. Double-wrap in plastic bags. Bring to room temperature before serving. If sticky, bake on foil-lined jelly roll pan in 250°F oven until crisp, about 20 minutes.*)

Garlic Almonds

Makes 1 pound

1 tablespoon unsalted butter
2 tablespoons soy sauce
2 teaspoons hot pepper sauce
3 garlic cloves, mashed

1 pound blanched whole almonds
3 teaspoons seasoned pepper
1/4 teaspoon dried red pepper flakes
Salt

Preheat oven to 350°F. Coat rimmed baking sheet with 1 tablespoon butter. Sprinkle with soy sauce, hot pepper sauce and garlic. Scatter almonds over sheet and stir with fork until well coated. Sprinkle with 1 1/2 teaspoons seasoned pepper, dried pepper flakes and salt. Bake 10 minutes. Sprinkle almonds with remaining seasoned pepper and additional salt if desired. Stir with fork. Bake 15 minutes. Cool before serving. (*Garlic Almonds can be stored in airtight container for up to 3 months.*)

Rosemary Roasted Walnuts

These spiced nuts also add a delicious touch to tossed green salads.

Makes about 2 cups

1/4 cup (1/2 stick) well-chilled unsalted butter, cut into 4 pieces
1 tablespoon dried rosemary, crumbled

1/4 teaspoon salt
1/8 teaspoon cayenne pepper
2 cups walnut halves (8 ounces)

Position rack in center of oven and preheat to 400°F. Line jelly roll pan with foil. Combine butter, rosemary, salt and cayenne in pan. Place in oven; melt butter. Add walnuts and toss to coat. Bake until walnuts are lightly toasted, stirring every 3 minutes, 6 to 9 minutes. Cool completely. (*Can be prepared 10 days ahead. Store in airtight container. Recrisp in 400°F oven 5 minutes.*)

Cheese-Garlic Popcorn

4 to 6 servings

2 teaspoons salt
1 teaspoon garlic powder
1/2 teaspoon onion powder
1/4 teaspoon ground oregano

1/4 cup grated Romano cheese
1/4 cup grated Parmesan cheese
3 1/2 quarts freshly made popcorn

Combine first 4 ingredients in small jar and shake well to blend. Mix cheeses in large bowl. Add popcorn and seasonings and toss well. Serve immediately.

Coconut Granola

Fill a canister or decorative storage jar with this mixture to present as a perfect hostess gift.

6 servings

1 medium coconut

4½ teaspoons grated orange peel

½ cup firmly packed dark brown sugar

¾ cup (1½ sticks) unsalted butter, melted

¼ cup pure maple syrup

1 teaspoon cinnamon

¼ teaspoon freshly grated nutmeg

1⅓ cups rolled oats

4 ounces wheat flakes*

4 ounces barley flakes*

4 ounces rye flakes*

½ cup blanched whole almonds

½ cup dry-roasted cashews

Preheat oven to 400°F. Pierce holes through coconut at 3 soft spots on one end using hammer and nail. Drain liquid. Bake coconut until shell cracks, about 20 minutes. Cool slightly. Wrap in towel. Sharply pound center of coconut with hammer to crack open. Separate meat from shell. Remove brown skin using vegetable peeler. Cut coconut into feed-tube widths.

Insert fine shredder into processor. Arrange coconut in feed tube and shred using firm pressure. Transfer ⅔ cup coconut to 2½-quart bowl. (*Remainder can be frozen 6 months. Thaw at room temperature.*)

Position rack in center of oven. Reduce temperature to 300°F. Line 2 jelly roll pans with aluminum foil.

Mince orange peel with sugar in processor, about 1 minute. Add butter, maple syrup, cinnamon and nutmeg and blend 5 seconds. Add peel mixture to coconut with all remaining ingredients; toss thoroughly. Transfer to prepared pans, spreading evenly. Bake until dry, stirring every 10 minutes, about 45 minutes. Cool completely before serving. (*Can be prepared 2 weeks ahead. Store in airtight container.*)

*Available at natural foods stores.

2 ❦ Pâtés, Sausages and Meat Pies

What could make a more elegant or impressive gift than a freshly made pâté, covered with a shiny aspic and presented in a French country basket with jars of traditional cornichons, pickled onions and a loaf of crusty bread? The wonderful surprise in this chapter is that many of the pâtés, such as Herbed Veal and Pork Pâté with Pistachios (page 12) and Terrine of Beef and Veal with Whole Mushrooms (page 12), are simple to make, and all can be done ahead of time; in fact, most pâtés and terrines benefit from being fixed a few days in advance to allow the flavors to mellow.

For an equally distinctive but more rustic presentation, make a batch of sausages or meat pies to be served at breakfast or for supper. Garlicky Homemade Red Wine Sausages (page 8) and Smoked Chorizo (page 8) would be a welcome addition to a festive barbecue. And Roast Pork and Apple Breakfast Pies (page 10), with their special pastry decoration, are a perfect year-round gift.

When packaging gifts made with meat, remember to include instructions for storage, cooking and serving. Use attractive, reusable crocks, tins and molds for pâtés and terrines. Wrap sausages in a handsome wooden bowl with good "go-withs" such as fresh pasta, extra-thick English muffins, smoked cheeses or an array of brightly colored bell peppers. Remember to keep meats chilled until they are ready to be transported.

Homemade Red Wine Sausages

These zesty sausages are redolent of garlic.

Makes about 18

9 feet sausage casings*

3 pounds pork butt, cut into
   1½-inch cubes

¾ cup Italian dry red wine

3 tablespoons minced fresh Italian
   parsley

4 teaspoons minced garlic

3½ teaspoons salt

1⅛ teaspoons freshly ground pepper

Rinse casings under cold water. Soak in cold water to cover 1 hour, changing water occasionally.

Mix all remaining ingredients.

Rinse casings. Slip one end of casing over faucet and run cold water through. Clip out or tie any sections with holes. Blot dry. Fit meat grinder with coarse blade. Attach stuffing horn to grinder. Place one end of casing over horn. Gradually push casing onto horn, leaving 1-inch overhang. Tie knot in end with fine string. With right hand feed sausage mixture through meat grinder while anchoring casing to horn with left thumb, allowing casing to unroll as mixture is extruded. Twist and tie with string at 4-inch intervals. Remove from horn and tie knot in end of casing. Cut sausage into links. (*Can be prepared ahead and refrigerated 2 days or frozen 1 month. Thaw sausage before cooking.*)

To cook, pierce sausage with fork and grill on barbecue or over indoor grill until cooked through, turning occasionally, about 10 minutes. Serve hot.

*Available at specialty markets and butcher supply stores.

Smoked Chorizo

Makes about 5 pounds

5 pounds untrimmed boned pork
   shoulder, cut into 1-inch cubes

3 tablespoons red chili powder

3 tablespoons salt

2 tablespoons hot paprika

1 tablespoon minced garlic

1 tablespoon dried red chili flakes

1 teaspoon dried oregano,
   crumbled

8 to 10 feet hog sausage casings

1 tablespoon distilled white vinegar

¼ cup tequila or water

3 tablespoons red wine vinegar

Mesquite chips, soaked in water
30 minutes and drained

Combine pork, chili powder, salt, paprika, garlic, chili flakes and oregano in large bowl. Cover mixture and marinate in refrigerator overnight.

Soak casings in cold water mixed with distilled vinegar 1 hour. Rinse. Slip one end of casing over faucet and run cold water through. Clip out or tie closed any sections with holes. Soak in cold water while preparing filling.

Coarsely grind pork mixture in meat grinder or processor. Return to bowl. Make well in center of meat mixture. Add tequila and red wine vinegar to well; knead into meat.

Attach stuffing horn to grinder (casings can also be stuffed with pastry bag fitted with ½-inch plain tip). Wring out casings and place one end over horn. Gradually push all of casing onto horn, leaving 6-inch overhang. Tie knot in overhang. With right hand, feed meat mixture into grinder. Meanwhile, anchor casing on top of horn with left thumb, allowing casing to unroll as mixture is extruded. Stop occasionally to mold meat. Pierce any air bubbles with fine needle. Do not pack too full or sausage will burst as filling expands during cooking.

Remove horn and knot casing. Knot 3-inch pieces of string around sausages at 4-inch intervals. Cut into individual sausages. Place on paper-towel-lined pan. Refrigerate uncovered overnight.

Prepare barbecue grill. Fold heavy-duty foil to form tray. Place on grill rack; add sausage to tray. Add mesquite to grill. Cover grill and cook sausage over low heat until firm to touch, about 25 minutes. (*Smoked Chorizo can be prepared 1 month ahead and refrigerated or 3 months ahead and frozen.*)

Herbed Sausage

A fine mild sausage. Use the food processor to make sausages quickly and simply. The cheesecloth wrapping eliminates the need for casings or special stuffing equipment.

Makes 9 sausages

1½ cups fresh parsley leaves
2 large shallots
2 large garlic cloves
2 slices firm white bread, broken into 6 pieces
2 tablespoons nonfat dry milk powder
1 tablespoon Seasoning Salt*
¾ teaspoon coarsely ground pepper
1¼ pounds lean pork loin (semifrozen), cut into 1-inch cubes
¾ pound pork fat (semifrozen), cut into 1-inch cubes

6 quarts water
1 large carrot, cut into 3 pieces
1 medium onion, pierced with 2 cloves
8 parsley sprigs
2 bay leaves
½ teaspoon dried thyme, crumbled

Mince parsley finely in processor work bowl using on/off turns. With machine running, drop shallots and garlic through feed tube and process until finely minced. Add bread, milk powder, Seasoning Salt and pepper and blend until bread is finely chopped, about 10 seconds. Remove ⅔ of mixture from work bowl and set aside. Add ⅓ *each* of pork loin and pork fat to work bowl and chop using 4 on/off turns, then blend until meat is finely ground, about 30 seconds. Remove from work bowl. Repeat with remaining bread and meat mixtures, processing in 2 additional batches.

Using 4 ounces of mixture for each sausage, shape into 9 cylinders about 4 inches long and 1¼ inches thick. Wrap each in double thickness of fine-mesh cheesecloth. Tie ends with string.

Combine water, carrot, onion and herbs in 8-quart stockpot and bring to boil over high heat. Add sausages, reduce heat to medium-low and simmer until internal temperature of sausages reaches 160°F, about 25 minutes. Remove using slotted spoon. Let cool in cheesecloth to prevent sausages from drying. Unwrap just before serving. Serve at room temperature or chilled.

*Seasoning Salt

Makes about ⅓ cup

¼ cup salt
1 teaspoon dried tarragon, crumbled
1 teaspoon Hungarian sweet paprika
1 teaspoon ground allspice

1 teaspoon ground coriander
½ teaspoon cinnamon
½ teaspoon freshly grated nutmeg
¼ teaspoon dried marjoram, crumbled
⅛ teaspoon ground cloves

Combine all ingredients in small jar and shake well. Store in cool place.

Roast Pork and Apple Breakfast Pies

A great use for leftover roast pork. Pork shoulder will give the most succulent filling. Decorate each pie with the recipient's initials for a charming gift.

Makes 12

Pastry
7 1/2 cups unbleached all purpose flour
   4 teaspoons salt
   2 teaspoons dried sage, crumbled
   2 teaspoons grated lemon peel
   1 cup (2 sticks) well-chilled unsalted butter
   1 cup well-chilled solid vegetable shortening
 2/3 to 1 cup ice water

Pork and Apple Filling
   2 tablespoons (1/4 stick) unsalted butter
   3 medium leeks (white part only), coarsely sliced
   2 cups coarsely chopped onion
   2 large Golden Delicious apples, peeled, cored and cut into 1/2-inch dice

   2 tablespoons minced fresh sage
   1 teaspoon dried thyme, crumbled

2 1/4 cups 1/2-inch-dice roast pork shoulder
   3 tablespoons dry breadcrumbs
   3 tablespoons whipping cream
 1/4 teaspoon (scant) ground allspice
      Salt and freshly ground pepper

   2 eggs beaten with 4 teaspoons water (glaze)

  24 fresh sage leaves

For pastry: Combine flour, salt, sage and lemon peel in large bowl. Cut in butter and shortening until coarse meal forms. Add enough water to form stiff dough that pulls away from sides of bowl. Gather into 2 rounds; flatten into discs. Wrap each in waxed paper. Refrigerate at least 3 hours or overnight.

For filling: Melt butter in heavy large skillet over medium heat. Add leeks and cook until beginning to soften, stirring occasionally, about 5 minutes. Add onion, increase heat to medium-high and stir until onion begins to soften, about 3 minutes. Mix in apples, sage and thyme. Cool completely.

Let pastry stand at room temperature 20 minutes before rolling.

Stir all remaining ingredients except glaze and sage into apple mixture.

Preheat oven to 400°F. Line baking sheets with parchment. Roll 1 piece of dough out on lightly floured surface to thickness of 1/8 inch. Cut out six 6-inch rounds, using plate as guide. Repeat with second piece of dough. Reserve any scraps. Spoon 1/2 cup filling onto left half of 1 dough round, leaving 1-inch border. Brush border with glaze. Fold right half of dough over filling, then press and crimp edges to seal. Transfer to prepared sheet. Repeat with remaining pastry.

Roll dough scraps out on lightly floured surface to thickness of 1/8 inch. Cut out initial or other design. Brush pies with glaze. Place initial in center of each pie. Garnish with sage leaves. Brush initial and leaves with glaze. Make 3 steam holes in each pie using skewer. Bake 10 minutes. Reduce temperature to 350°F and continue baking until pies are rich golden brown and bubbling juices appear around steam holes, covering loosely with foil if browning too quickly, 25 to 30 minutes. Cool slightly on rack. (*Can be prepared 1 day ahead and refrigerated. Reheat pies in 350°F oven 5 to 7 minutes.*)

Spinach Pâté

18 appetizer servings

1 cup dried chick-peas, soaked in cold water overnight

3 tablespoons light vegetable oil (preferably cold-pressed safflower)

1/4 cup whole wheat pastry flour

2 tablespoons unflavored gelatin

1 cup milk *or* reconstituted nonfat dry milk

2 pounds fresh spinach, well washed and trimmed

1/2 cup chopped shallot

1/2 cup packed fresh basil leaves

1/2 cup soft whole wheat breadcrumbs or cubes

3 egg yolks

2 teaspoons chopped fresh garlic

2 teaspoons herb or vegetable salt (or to taste)

1/2 cup pine nuts, toasted, or coarsely chopped walnuts

6 whole wheat lasagne strips (about)

1 bunch fresh parsley (garnish) Cherry tomatoes

Combine chick-peas and soaking liquid in large saucepan. Cover and cook over medium-high heat until tender, about 3 1/2 hours. Drain; reserve 3/4 cup cooking liquid. Transfer chick-peas to processor. Add 1/4 cup cooking liquid and puree mixture until smooth.

Bring remaining 1/2 cup chick-pea cooking liquid and 2 tablespoons vegetable oil to boil over medium heat in small saucepan. Remove from heat. Combine flour and gelatin in small bowl. Add to cooking liquid and stir until smooth. Blend in milk. Return to heat and stir until mixture comes to boil and thickens. Freeze until just set, about 7 to 10 minutes.

Place spinach in large saucepan and sprinkle with water. Cover and cook over medium-high heat, turning spinach occasionally until just wilted, about 2 to 3 minutes. Drain spinach in colander, pressing out as much liquid as possible (if necessary, squeeze spinach dry between paper towels). Transfer to processor and puree, or press through fine grinder. Add chick-pea puree, shallot, basil, breadcrumbs, egg yolks and garlic and puree until smooth. Add gelatin mixture and mix well. Season with herb salt. Transfer mixture to large bowl. Fold in nuts.

Preheat oven to 350°F. Cook lasagne in boiling water with remaining 1 tablespoon vegetable oil for 10 minutes. Drain well; rinse under cold water and drain again. Spread strips on paper towels and pat dry. Coat 2-quart pâté mold or 9 × 5-inch loaf pan with oil. Line mold with lasagne strips, extending over sides. Fill with spinach mixture. Fold ends of lasagne strips over top. If necessary, cover with remaining strips. Cover top of mold tightly with waxed paper and then aluminum foil, crimping edges to make tight seal. Set mold in roasting pan. Pour in enough hot water to come halfway up sides of mold. Bake 1 1/2 hours. Remove mold from pan but do not unwrap. Let cool slightly. Weight with heavy object (a brick covered with aluminum foil works well). Let cool to room temperature. Refrigerate at least 12 hours. (*Pâté can be refrigerated up to 1 week.*)

To serve, invert pâté onto large serving platter (if necessary, dip pan in hot water 1 minute to loosen). Surround with parsley sprigs and cherry tomatoes.

Herbed Veal and Pork Pâté with Pistachios

Wrap up a crock of this delicious, easy-to-make pâté in a basket with cornichons, pickled onions, French bread and a tub of sweet butter.

12 servings

1 tablespoon butter
1 large onion, chopped

1/2 pound chicken livers
1/2 pound finely ground lean pork
1/2 pound finely ground veal
1/2 pound finely ground pork fat
1/4 pound smoked ham, cut into 1/3-inch pieces
1/2 cup whipping cream
1/4 cup Cognac
1/4 cup husked pistachio nuts (optional)
2 eggs, beaten to blend
2 teaspoons salt

1 1/2 teaspoon minced garlic
1 teaspoon freshly ground pepper
1/4 teaspoon ground allspice
1/4 teaspoon mace
1/4 teaspoon dried rosemary, crumbled
1/4 teaspoon dried thyme, crumbled
1/8 teaspoon ground cloves
Several dashes of cayenne pepper
1 large bay leaf, halved
Parsley sprigs

Preheat oven to 350°F. Melt butter in heavy medium skillet over medium heat. Add onion and cook until golden brown, about 10 minutes. Cool.

Finely chop half of chicken livers; puree remainder. Transfer to large bowl. Add onion and all remaining ingredients except bay leaf and parsley. Mix well. Spoon into 8-cup oval or rectangular terrine. Insert bay leaf half into each end. Cover terrine. Place in baking pan. Pour enough hot water into baking pan to come halfway up sides of terrine. Bake 2 hours. Uncover and continue baking until thermometer inserted in center registers 190°F and pâté browns and begins to pull away from sides of terrine, about 20 minutes. Remove terrine from water. Top pâté with foil, then with heavy object; cool completely. Remove weight and refrigerate pâté overnight. (*Can be prepared 5 days ahead.*) Remove pâté from pan and discard bay leaves. Let stand at room temperature 1 hour before serving. Garnish with parsley.

Terrine of Beef and Veal with Whole Mushrooms

For maximum flavor, make this easy pâté two to three days ahead.

12 servings

2 tablespoons (1/4 stick) butter
3/4 pound 1-inch mushrooms, stems removed
1/2 cup minced onion
1/4 cup Cognac
2 tablespoons minced fresh oregano or 1 teaspoon dried, crumbled
3 large garlic cloves, minced
1/4 cup sour cream
Salt and freshly ground pepper

4 to 6 bacon strips
1/3 cup half and half

2 eggs
2 cups fresh breadcrumbs
1 1/2 pounds ground beef chuck
3/4 pound ground veal
1/4 cup minced fresh parsley
1 teaspoon minced orange peel

Tomato Macadamia Nut Chutney (see page 46)

Melt butter in heavy large skillet over medium-high heat. Add mushrooms, onion, Cognac, oregano and garlic and cook until liquid evaporates, stirring occasionally, about 7 minutes. Add sour cream and cook 2 minutes to blend flavors. Season generously with salt and freshly ground pepper.

Preheat oven to 375°F. Line bottom of 6-cup terrine mold with bacon. Whisk half and half and eggs in large bowl. Stir in breadcrumbs. Combine chuck, veal, parsley and orange peel in another bowl. Season generously with salt and pepper.

Blend in breadcrumb mixture. Pat half of meat mixture into prepared mold. Make trough down center. Arrange mushrooms in trough. Cover with remaining meat mixture, smoothing top. Bake 1¹/₂ hours. Let terrine stand 30 minutes.

Preheat broiler. Pour off fat from mold. Invert terrine onto baking sheet. Broil terrine until bacon crisps. Cool completely. Wrap in foil and refrigerate 2 to 3 days. Cut into thin slices. Serve with chutney.

Veal and Apple Terrine with Green Peppercorns and Calvados

10 servings

Terrine
- 3 tablespoons unsalted butter
- 1 pound Golden Delicious apples, peeled, cored and cut into ¹/₃-inch dice
- 1 large onion, diced

- 2 pounds ground veal
- 4 eggs
- ³/₄ cup dry breadcrumbs
- ¹/₃ cup dried currants
- ¹/₃ cup Calvados or applejack
- ¹/₃ cup dry Marsala
- 2 tablespoons plus 1¹/₂ teaspoons green peppercorns packed in brine, drained

- 2 tablespoons dried tarragon, crumbled
- 2 teaspoons dried thyme, crumbled
- 2 teaspoons fresh lemon juice
- 2 teaspoons salt
- 1 teaspoon grated lemon peel Freshly ground pepper

Garnish
- Calvados Gelée*
- 5 to 6 paper-thin apple slices
- 2 to 3 fresh tarragon sprigs
- 1 to 2 fresh thyme sprigs
- 2 teaspoons green peppercorns packed in brine, rinsed and drained

For terrine: Position rack in center of oven and preheat to 350°F. Melt butter in heavy large skillet over medium heat. Add apples and onion. Cook until tender, stirring frequently, about 10 minutes. Cool completely.

Combine apple mixture with all remaining ingredients in large bowl of heavy-duty electric mixer. Using dough hook on low speed, mix until well combined, about 4 to 5 minutes. Pack mixture lightly into 2- to 2¹/₂-quart deep oval terrine or loaf pan. Smooth top with rubber spatula. Bake until terrine is brown and pulling away from sides of pan, about 1¹/₂ hours. Cool on rack. Wipe edges of pan. Refrigerate until well chilled. (*Can be prepared 1 day ahead.*)

For garnish: Ladle ¹/₈-inch-thick layer of gelée over cold terrine. Arrange apples, herbs and peppercorns decoratively atop gelée. Refrigerate until gelée is very firm, 20 to 30 minutes.

If remaining gelée has solidified, soften over low heat, stirring constantly. Cool until starting to thicken, stirring frequently. Ladle over terrine, tipping pan to spread evenly. Refrigerate until firm. (*Can be prepared 1 day ahead.*) Let stand at room temperature 1 hour before serving.

*Calvados Gelée

Makes about 2 cups

- 1 tablespoon unflavored gelatin
- 1³/₄ cups well-strained rich veal or beef stock

- ¹/₄ cup Calvados or applejack
- 1 teaspoon fresh lemon juice

Sprinkle gelatin over ¹/₂ cup stock in small cup. Combine remaining 1¹/₄ cup stock, Calvados and lemon juice in heavy nonaluminum saucepan. Bring to simmer. Add gelatin to stock mixture, stirring until gelatin dissolves. Cool until mixture is room temperature, stirring frequently.

Pâté de Campagne

A classic French country pâté, flecked with smoked ham for extra flavor and texture. Prepare it several days ahead to give the flavors a chance to mingle and mellow.

8 to 10 servings

1 small onion, quartered
2 large garlic cloves
1 pound turkey breast (uncooked), cut into 1-inch cubes
8 ounces slab bacon (rind removed), cut into 1-inch cubes
2 chicken livers
2 eggs
1/4 cup Cognac
3/4 teaspoon cinnamon
1/2 teaspoon salt

1/4 teaspoon freshly grated nutmeg
Freshly ground pepper
4 ounces imported smoked ham, cut into 1/8-inch cubes

Cornichons or other small sour pickles (thinly sliced lengthwise), radish roses and parsley sprigs (garnishes)

Position rack in center of oven and preheat to 350°F. Butter 1-quart terrine or loaf pan. Butter foil to cover terrine.

With machine running, drop onion and garlic through processor feed tube and mince finely. Add turkey, bacon and chicken livers to work bowl and chop using about 6 on/off turns, then blend until smooth, about 1 minute. Add eggs, Cognac and seasoning and process 10 seconds, stopping once to scrape down sides of work bowl. Add ham and mix using several on/off turns; do not overprocess. (To check seasoning, form about 2 tablespoons of mixture into small patty. Melt small amount of butter in small skillet over medium heat. Add patty and sauté until cooked through, then taste and adjust seasoning of remaining mixture.)

Transfer contents of work bowl to prepared terrine, smoothing surface with spatula. Cover terrine with prepared foil. Bake until internal temperature reaches 160°F, about 1 1/2 hours. Remove from oven and top with weight. Let cool; drain if necessary. Chill. (*Can be prepared several days ahead and refrigerated.*)

To serve, loosen pâté from pan using flexible-bladed spatula. Invert onto platter. Surround with fans of sliced pickles, radish roses and parsley.

Terrine à l'Orange

10 to 12 servings

1/2 pound boned, skinned chicken thigh meat, cut into large pieces
1/2 pound chicken livers
1/4 cup brandy
1/4 cup orange juice

2 tablespoons (1/4 stick) butter
3 medium onions, chopped

1 1/2 pounds pork shoulder, cut into 2-inch cubes
1 pound pork fat, cubed
1 1 1/2-pound whole chicken breast, skinned, boned and cubed

2 eggs
1/4 cup whipping cream
2 tablespoons Terrine Spice*
1 tablespoon grated orange peel

1 pound pork fatback, thinly sliced

2 bay leaves
2 whole cloves

1 teaspoon gelatin
1 tablespoon cold water
2 medium oranges (unpeeled), sliced

Combine chicken thigh meat, chicken livers, brandy and orange juice in medium bowl. Refrigerate overnight.

Remove chicken livers from marinade; drain on paper towels. Melt butter in heavy medium skillet over medium heat. Add livers and sauté until firm but still pink inside, 3 to 4 minutes. Transfer to small bowl using slotted spoon. Add onions to skillet and sauté until tender, 8 to 9 minutes. Set aside.

Remove half of chicken thigh meat from marinade; drain on paper towels. Transfer to processor. Add onions, pork, pork fat and chicken breast meat and chop coarsely, using on/off turns. Transfer to large bowl. Add eggs, cream, Terrine Spice and orange peel. Beat with wooden spoon until thoroughly combined. Cover tightly and refrigerate overnight. (Refrigerate remaining thigh meat, in marinade, and sautéed livers separately.)

Remove remaining chicken thigh meat from marinade; drain on paper towels. Cut into 4 × 1-inch strips. Reserve 6 chicken livers. Finely chop remaining liver and add to chopped meat mixture. Blend in marinade.

Line 8-cup terrine or 9 × 5 × 3-inch loaf pan with fatback, leaving 3- to 4-inch overhang. Spoon ⅓ of meat mixture into terrine. Top with fatback slices. Arrange reserved chicken livers in row down center, then wrap with fatback from underneath. Add ⅓ of meat mixture, pressing down lightly. Top with fatback slices. Arrange thigh meat strips in row down center, then wrap with fatback from underneath. Top with remaining meat mixture, mounding slightly and smoothing evenly with wet spatula.

Preheat oven to 350°F. Press bay leaves and cloves onto top of terrine. Fold fatback overhang over top, adding more fatback if necessary to cover. Cover terrine with foil. Place in roasting pan. Transfer to oven. Add enough boiling water to roasting pan to come halfway up sides of terrine. Bake until thermometer inserted into center of terrine registers 170°F or until juices run yellow with no trace of pink, about 2 hours and 50 minutes, adding more boiling water to roasting pan if necessary. Transfer terrine to wire rack and remove foil. Cool completely. Pour juices off top of terrine into measuring cup. Cover terrine with foil and weight with heavy object. Refrigerate overnight. Cover juices and refrigerate overnight.

Remove fatback from top of loaf. Remove fat from juices. Add water if necessary to measure ⅔ cup liquid. Bring to boil in small saucepan.

Meanwhile, soften gelatin in 1 tablespoon cold water 5 minutes. Add to boiling juices and stir until dissolved. Strain through cheesecloth-lined sieve into small bowl. Place bowl in another bowl of ice water and cool glaze until slightly syrupy. Arrange orange slices down center of terrine. Brush or spoon glaze evenly over oranges. Refrigerate until set. Serve chilled.

*Terrine Spice

This recipe makes more spice mixture than you will need. Try the remainder in meat loaf or hamburgers or sprinkle on grilled chicken.

Makes 1 ³/₄ cups

1 **cup salt**	1 **tablespoon dried basil, crumbled**
2 **tablespoons cinnamon**	2 **teaspoons Spanish paprika**
1 **tablespoon crushed bay leaf**	1½ **teaspoons ground cloves**
1 **tablespoon ground thyme**	1 **teaspoon freshly ground white**
1 **tablespoon ground mace**	**pepper**
1 **tablespoon dried rosemary, crumbled**	½ **teaspoon ground allspice**

Grind all ingredients in mortar with pestle or in blender or coffee grinder.

Terrine of Rabbit

For maximum flavor, prepare this spicy loaf two to three days ahead.

12 servings

1 3-pound rabbit, heart and liver reserved

1 pound dark chicken meat
5 ounces dry salami
1 medium onion, sliced
1 garlic clove, minced
2/3 cup Zinfandel or other dry red wine
1/4 cup brandy
2 tablespoons minced fresh parsley
1 tablespoon olive oil
1 1/2 teaspoons salt
1 teaspoon dried oregano, crumbled
1/2 teaspoon ground pepper

3/4 pound sliced bacon
3 ounces dry breadcrumbs
2 ounces shelled, unroasted pistachio nuts, coarsely chopped
2 eggs, beaten to blend
4 parsley sprigs
1 bay leaf
   Italian parsley

Bone rabbit. Cut flanks from each side of back and meat from back legs into 1/2-inch-thick slices. Do not cut remaining meat. Wrap and refrigerate overnight.

Grind remaining rabbit meat, reserved heart and liver, chicken, salami, onion and garlic through medium plate of meat grinder into large bowl. Blend wine, brandy, parsley, oil, salt, oregano and pepper in another bowl. Stir into meat mixture. Cover and refrigerate overnight.

Preheat oven to 325°F. Line bottom and sides of 9 × 5-inch loaf pan with bacon. Mix breadcrumbs, pistachios and eggs. Beat into meat mixture. Press half of mixture into prepared pan. Top with rabbit slices. Cover with remaining meat mixture. Tap on counter to eliminate air pockets. Decorate with parsley and bay leaf. Fold bacon over to cover completely. Set in roasting pan. Add enough simmering water to roasting pan to come halfway up sides of loaf pan. Bake until terrine is firm and juices run clear, about 2 hours. Top terrine with weight. Cool completely. Remove weight. Refrigerate until ready to serve. Invert terrine onto platter. Garnish with Italian parsley.

3 🍏 Sauces, Salad Dressings and Seasonings

Nothing dresses up a dish as much as a special sauce, whether it's a family-recipe barbecue marinade or a simple hot fudge sauce laced with liqueur. Whatever the gift-giving season, a jar of homemade dressing or seasoning is as treasured as a secret shared among friends.

This chapter includes some of the easiest recipes for food gifts, such as Hot Peppered Old South Vinegar (page 27) and Lime Mustard (page 31). Some of them require a bit of standing time to bring out their best flavor, such as Brandied Vanilla Essence (page 25) and Basic Fruit Vinegar (page 27), but they are not at all complicated. Note that almost all sauces should be kept refrigerated, but many are served warm. In the gift package, include instructions for storing and serving.

Because these specialties are so quick to make, you can spend more time packaging them creatively. Put Fresh Basil Vinegar (page 26) into an unusually shaped bottle sealed with colored wax and tied at the neck with a bundle of dried herbs. Present sauces and dressings like Poppy Seed Dressing (page 30) or Cumberland Sauce (page 20) in stoneware jugs with tight-fitting lids, or in fancy canning jars. Decorate your own gift tags and be sure to include serving ideas with perhaps a favorite recipe using the sauce or seasoning.

 Savory Sauces

Genoese Red Pesto

A piquant and colorful pesto that is a refreshing dressing for summer salads, chicken, fish and rare roast beef.

Makes 4 cups

2 medium-size ripe tomatoes
³/4 pound red bell peppers
4 anchovies, drained
¹/4 teaspoon salt
1 large garlic clove
¹/2 cup pine nuts, toasted
1¹/2 cups fresh white breadcrumbs

¹/3 cup red wine vinegar
4 teaspoons capers, rinsed and drained
1 tablespoon fresh parsley leaves
1 tablespoon fresh oregano leaves
²/3 cup olive oil

Preheat broiler. Roast tomatoes and peppers 2 inches from heat source until tomatoes are lightly charred and peppers are blistered and charred, turning often. Steam peppers 10 minutes in plastic bag. Peel and seed. Rinse; pat dry. Peel and seed tomatoes.

Blend anchovies, salt and garlic in processor to paste. Add pine nuts and mix using on/off turns, scraping down sides of bowl. Mix in peppers and tomatoes, scraping down sides of bowl. Blend in breadcrumbs, vinegar, capers, parsley and oregano. With machine running, slowly add olive oil and mix until thick. Transfer to jar; seal tightly. Refrigerate at least 2 hours. (*Can be prepared 2 weeks ahead.*) Serve at room temperature.

Cilantro Pesto

Use as a seasoning for pasta or soups.

Makes about ³/4 cup

2 cups cilantro leaves
¹/2 cup freshly grated Parmesan cheese
¹/3 cup hulled pepitas (pumpkin seed)

¹/4 cup olive oil
2 tablespoons minced garlic
2 tablespoons fresh lime juice
¹/2 teaspoon salt

Grind all ingredients in processor or blender to paste, stopping occasionally to scrape down sides of work bowl. Store in airtight container. (*Can be prepared 5 days ahead and refrigerated.*)

Green Sauce

An easy no-cook sauce that is perfect with cold ham.

Makes about 1 cup

1 cup packed fresh spinach leaves
1 cup packed fresh parsley leaves
¹/2 cup packed fresh cilantro leaves
2 tablespoons capers, rinsed and drained
2 green onions (white part only), each cut crosswise into 3 pieces

1 large garlic clove
¹/2 cup olive oil
1¹/2 tablespoons red wine vinegar
¹/8 to ¹/4 teaspoon coarse salt
¹/8 teaspoon freshly ground black pepper
Dash of hot pepper sauce

Combine spinach, parsley, cilantro, 1 tablespoon capers, green onions and garlic in processor and mix using on/off turns until coarsely chopped, scraping down sides of bowl. With machine running, quickly pour in ⅓ cup oil. Pour mixture into small bowl. Whisk in remaining oil. Blend in vinegar, salt, pepper and hot pepper sauce. Stir in remaining capers. Cover and refrigerate until ready to serve.

Lemon-Mustard Sauce

Prepare this well in advance and serve with broiled lamb.

Makes about 1 cup

6 tablespoons (¾ stick) unsalted butter
2 large garlic cloves, minced
3 tablespoons coarse-ground French mustard (moutarde de meaux)
Shredded peel from 2 large lemons

Juice of 1 lemon
¼ teaspoon dried oregano (preferably Greek) or to taste
Salt and freshly ground pepper

Combine butter and garlic in small saucepan and cook over low heat 3 to 5 minutes. Just before serving, whisk in remaining ingredients; heat briefly.

Cold Mustard Sauce

This tangy sauce and the next two recipes are the perfect complement to oysters on the half shell.

Makes about 1½ cups

1 cup mayonnaise
¼ cup whipping cream
2 tablespoons chopped green onion
1 tablespoon chopped capers
1 tablespoon chopped fresh parsley
2 teaspoons coarse-grained French mustard

2 teaspoons fresh tarragon or ½ teaspoon dried, crumbled
2 teaspoons fresh lemon juice
1 teaspoon Worcestershire sauce
¼ teaspoon freshly ground pepper
Dash of hot pepper sauce

Whisk all ingredients in small bowl. Cover; refrigerate until ready to serve.

Pickled Pepper Sauce

Makes about 2 cups

2 cups fresh red or green chilies
2 garlic cloves, sliced

2 to 3 fresh dill sprigs
2 cups white vinegar

Combine chilies, garlic and dill in 1-quart jar. Bring vinegar to boil. Pour vinegar over chilies. Cover jar tightly. Let stand in cool place at least 2 days to mellow. To serve, strain sauce into small bowl; discard garlic and dill.

Black Pepper Sauce

Makes about 1½ cups

1 cup catsup
¼ cup water
2 tablespoons freshly ground pepper

1 tablespoon cider vinegar
1 tablespoon fresh lemon juice
1 teaspoon cayenne pepper
½ teaspoon salt

Mix all ingredients in small bowl. Cover; refrigerate until ready to serve.

Dijon Mayonnaise

Makes about 1³/₄ cups

1 egg
1 teaspoon fresh lemon juice
1 teaspoon red wine vinegar
1 teaspoon Dijon mustard
1 teaspoon salt
Freshly ground white pepper

1¹/₂ cups oil (preferably safflower combined with 3 tablespoons olive oil)

Using food processor, combine egg, lemon juice, vinegar, mustard, salt and pepper with 3 tablespoons oil in work bowl and blend 8 seconds. With machine running, slowly add remaining oil through feed tube in thin, steady stream (once mayonnaise has thickened, oil can be added more quickly). Adjust seasoning. Transfer to airtight jar and refrigerate until ready to use. (*Can be refrigerated up to 10 days.*)

Cumberland Sauce

This sauce goes well with lamb or duck.

Makes 1¹/₄ cups

¹/₂ cup ruby Port
¹/₂ cup fresh orange juice
¹/₄ cup fresh lemon juice
1 shallot, minced
²/₃ cup red currant jelly

1 teaspoon finely grated orange peel
¹/₂ teaspoon finely grated lemon peel
¹/₈ teaspoon cayenne pepper
¹/₈ teaspoon ground ginger

Bring Port, juices and shallot to boil and cook until reduced by half. Add jelly, peels, cayenne and ginger and cook until slightly thickened. Store chilled.

Sesame-Mustard Sauce

Makes about 1 cup

¹/₃ cup Dijon mustard
2 tablespoons honey
2 tablespoons tahini (sesame seed paste)
1 egg yolk

2 teaspoons white wine vinegar
2 teaspoons oriental sesame oil
¹/₂ teaspoon salt
¹/₂ cup safflower oil

Blend mustard, honey, tahini, yolk, vinegar, sesame oil and salt in processor for 30 seconds. With machine running, pour safflower oil through feed tube in thin stream and blend well. (*Can be prepared 1 week ahead. Cover and refrigerate.*) Serve at room temperature.

Chili Sauce

This sauce is delicious served with any meat.

Make about 6 pints

10 pounds ripe tomatoes, peeled and chopped
4 medium-size yellow onions, finely chopped
3 green bell peppers, seeded and finely chopped
3 red bell peppers, seeded and finely chopped
2 cups finely chopped celery

2 cups cider vinegar
2 tablespoons salt
1 teaspoon cinnamon
1 teaspoon ground cloves
1 teaspoon allspice
1 teaspoon freshly grated nutmeg
¹/₂ teaspoon dry mustard

1 cup sugar

Cook tomatoes in heavy 8-quart Dutch oven or stockpot over high heat for 30 minutes, stirring frequently. Reduce heat and continue cooking until tomatoes have reduced by about half. Stir in onion, peppers and celery. Add vinegar, salt and spices and blend well. Increase heat and bring to low boil. Let boil about 2 hours, stirring frequently to prevent burning.

Blend in sugar and continue cooking until mixture is thick, about 30 minutes. Ladle into sterilized pint jars and seal. Store jars in cool, dark place.

Rancho Mole Sauce

This rich sauce refrigerates and freezes beautifully. In fact, it gets better as the flavors age and mellow. It really perks up grilled meats, poultry and sausages.

Makes about 10 cups

8 dried pasilla chilies*
6 dried pasilla negro chilies*
2 dried New Mexico or mulato chilies*

1/2 cup unblanched almonds
1/4 cup sesame seed
1/4 cup pine nuts
1 slice French bread, torn into pieces
1 corn tortilla

3 tablespoons raw pepitas (pumpkin seeds)
4 unpeeled garlic cloves

4 whole cloves
1 2-inch cinnamon stick

1 quart turkey or chicken stock
1 pound tomatoes, roasted, peeled and seeded
1/4 cup raisins, soaked in hot water until ready to use

3 tablespoons vegetable oil
3 tablespoons all purpose flour
1 to 2 3.3-ounce rounds Mexican chocolate*

Stem, seed and devein chilies. Break up into pieces. Rinse under cold water. Place in large metal bowl. Cover with boiling water. Cover tightly with foil. Let steep 1 to 2 hours.

Preheat oven to 350°F. Arrange almonds, sesame seed, pine nuts, bread and tortilla on baking sheets. Toast until golden brown, about 10 minutes.

Place pepitas in heavy small skillet over medium heat and toast well, about 2 minutes (watch carefully, pepitas may pop out of skillet). Remove from skillet. Add garlic to skillet and toast, tossing mixture occasionally, about 4 minutes.

Grind almonds to powder in spice mill or coffee grinder; transfer to bowl. Grind sesame seed to powder; transfer to bowl. Grind pine nuts, pepitas, cloves and cinnamon to powder; transfer to bowl. (Do not use processor for grinding; mixture will be gummy.)

Transfer 1/3 of chilies and 1/2 cup soaking liquid to blender and puree until smooth. Pour into large bowl. Repeat. Transfer remaining 1/3 of chilies, bread, tortilla and ground-nut mixture to blender. Add some of stock to moisten and puree until smooth. Pour some of mixture into bowl. Add undrained raisins, garlic and tomatoes to blender and puree until smooth. Pour pureed mixture into bowl. Stir well.

Heat oil in heavy large saucepan over medium-low heat. Whisk in flour and stir until golden, about 5 minutes. Add chili mixture. Stir in remaining stock 1/2 cup at a time and simmer 45 minutes to thicken and blend flavors.

Add 1 round of chocolate and simmer 15 minutes. Taste and add more chocolate if richer flavor is desired. Cool sauce completely. Cover and refrigerate until ready to serve. (*Can be prepared 1 week ahead and refrigerated.*)

*Available at Latin American markets.

Chunky Tomato Sauce

Serve this tasty vegetable sauce over spinach fettuccine or other pasta.

Makes 5 cups

1/4 cup (1/2 stick) butter
1 large onion, finely chopped
2 carrots, peeled and shredded
1 celery stalk, finely chopped
5 garlic cloves, finely chopped
1 28-ounce can tomatoes, seeded and chopped (juice reserved)
2 cups chicken broth
1 cup dry white wine
1/4 cup fresh lemon juice

1/4 cup fresh orange juice
1/4 cup chopped fresh parsley
1 teaspoon dried marjoram, crumbled
3/4 teaspoon salt
1/2 teaspoon dried basil, crumbled
1/2 teaspoon dried thyme, crumbled
1/2 teaspoon dried oregano, crumbled
Freshly ground pepper

Melt butter in Dutch oven over medium-low heat. Add onion, carrots, celery and garlic and sauté 10 minutes. Add remaining ingredients and bring to boil. Cook 10 minutes, stirring occasionally. Reduce heat and simmer until thickened, about 30 minutes. Serve tomato sauce hot. (*Can be prepared 1 week ahead, cooled and stored in refrigerator.*)

Barbecue Sauce and Marinade

This all-purpose sauce is great with broiled chicken breasts or flank steak.

Makes about 1 1/2 cups

1 tablespoon butter
1/2 onion, chopped
1/2 cup water
1/2 cup catsup

2 tablespoons brown sugar
1 1/2 tablespoon Worcestershire sauce
1 tablespoon cider vinegar
1 teaspoon dry mustard

Melt butter in medium skillet over medium-high heat. Add onion and sauté until tender, about 5 minutes. Blend in remaining ingredients. Cook until heated through, about 10 minutes. Let cool slightly. Transfer to jar and cover tightly. Store in refrigerator.

 # Sweet Sauces

Japanese Kumquat Sauce

This is a delightful topping for ice cream, waffles or crepes. Adding 1 1/2 ounces more pectin will make the sauce firm to a marmalade-like consistency.

Makes about 5 cups

1 pound kumquats, halved and seeded
2 1/2 cups cold water
2 tablespoons saké

1/4 cup fresh lemon juice
3 cups sugar
2 3-ounce pouches liquid pectin

Coarsely chop kumquats in processor using 1 or 2 on/off turns. Bring to boil with water and saké in heavy large saucepan. Reduce heat and simmer 2 minutes. Add lemon juice. Stir in sugar in 2 additions. Simmer 2 minutes. Increase heat and bring to rolling boil. Mix in pectin. Boil exactly 3 minutes, stirring occasionally. Immediately ladle sauce into sterilized jars and seal according to manufacturer's instructions. Refrigerate up to 6 months.

Spicy Apple Syrup

For serving warm over ice cream, pancakes or crepes. Accompany a jar of this syrup with a crepe pan for a perfect gift.

Makes about 1¹/₂ cups

1 cup cold water
1 6-ounce can frozen unsweetened apple juice concentrate, thawed
¹/₄ cup sugar

1¹/₂ tablespoons cornstarch
¹/₂ teaspoon cinnamon
¹/₂ teaspoon vanilla

Combine first 6 ingredients in 1¹/₂-quart saucepan and stir over medium heat until mixture simmers and clears, about 10 to 12 minutes. Serve warm; refrigerate any remaining syrup in jar.

Gin and Juniper-Spiced Applesauce

Three different varieties of apples lend an intriguing flavor and texture to this applesauce. Delicious warm or chilled.

Makes about 2¹/₂ quarts

2 cups water
²/₃ cup dry vermouth or Sauternes
¹/₄ cup fresh lemon juice
2 pounds Rome Beauty apples
2 pounds Golden Delicious apples
2 pounds tart green apples such as pippin or Granny Smith

1²/₃ cups sugar
¹/₂ cup gin
1 tablespoon juniper berries, crushed and wrapped in cheesecloth
1 teaspoon grated lemon peel
¹/₂ teaspoon salt

Combine water, vermouth and lemon juice in large nonaluminum saucepan. Peel apples in long continuous strips, reserving peel. Core apples and cut into ¹/₂-inch pieces. Add apples and peel to saucepan. Bring to boil. Reduce heat, cover partially and simmer until apple pieces are very tender, 15 to 20 minutes. Discard peels.

Add all remaining ingredients to apples. Simmer uncovered until sauce mounds in spoon, stirring frequently and mashing apples against side of pan, 30 minutes to 1 hour depending on juiciness of apples. Cool to room temperature. Cover and refrigerate overnight. Discard juniper berries before serving.

Apricot Sauce

Serve this over rich vanilla ice cream for a special dessert.

Makes about 3 cups

2 cups water (or more)
8 ounces dried apricots (1¹/₂ generous cups)
1 cup sweet white wine

1 vanilla bean, split lengthwise
1 tablespoon fresh lemon juice or to taste

Combine 2 cups water, apricots, wine and vanilla bean in medium saucepan and bring to simmer over medium heat. Reduce heat to medium-low and simmer until apricots are tender, 35 to 40 minutes. Remove vanilla bean. Transfer mixture to processor or blender and puree until smooth; strain. Stir in lemon juice. Thin to desired consistency with additional water. Cover sauce and chill thoroughly before serving.

Spiked Pineapple Dessert Sauce

Perfect over ice cream,
pound cake or gingerbread.

Makes about 3 cups

1 cup pineapple juice
1/2 cup water
1/2 cup lightly packed brown sugar
1 tablespoon cornstarch
Pinch of salt
1/2 cup Drambuie
1/2 cup chopped dates

1/2 cup chopped canned pineapple,
drained
1/2 cup chopped pecans
2 tablespoons (1/4 stick) butter
1/4 teaspoon freshly grated nutmeg
1/8 teaspoon grated lemon peel

Combine juice, water, sugar, cornstarch and salt in medium saucepan over medium heat. Stir until smooth and thickened, about 7 minutes. Gradually add Drambuie. Bring to boil and continue boiling 1 minute. Add remaining ingredients and cook 1 more minute. Serve warm.

Southwest Caramel Sauce

Excellent atop ice cream,
crepes or poached pears.
Package the sauce and
pecan garnish separately
and include a tag with
rewarming tips.

Makes about 3 1/4 cups

4 cups milk
2 1/2 cups whipping cream (preferably not ultra-pasteurized)
1 1/2 cups sugar
1 teaspoon cornstarch
1/2 teaspoon baking soda
1 tablespoon vanilla

2 tablespoons (1/4 stick) unsalted butter
1 1/2 cups chopped pecans

6 tablespoons (about) coffee liqueur (optional)
3/4 to 1 1/2 cups whipping cream

Whisk first 5 ingredients in heavy 3-quart saucepan. Bring to boil. Reduce heat and simmer until very thick and caramel color, about 3 1/2 hours. Stir in vanilla. Cool completely. Refrigerate.

Melt butter in heavy medium skillet over medium heat. Add pecans and stir until toasted, 3 to 4 minutes. Drain thoroughly on paper towels.

Just before serving, rewarm sauce in top of double boiler over simmering water, stirring occasionally. Thin each cup of sauce with 2 tablespoons liqueur (if desired) and 1/4 to 1/2 cup cream. Serve with toasted pecans.

Hot Fudge Sauce

This thick sauce has an
intense chocolate flavor and
silken texture.

Makes about 1 3/4 cups

1 1/4 cups sugar
4 ounces unsweetened chocolate, broken into pieces
1/4 cup (1/2 stick) unsalted butter, cut into 2 pieces, room temperature

1/2 cup milk, heated to simmer
1 tablespoon vanilla
1 teaspoon baking powder
Pinch of salt

Combine sugar and chocolate in processor work bowl and mix using 6 on/off turns, then process until chocolate is as fine as sugar, about 1 minute. With machine running, pour hot milk through feed tube and blend until chocolate is melted, about 30 seconds, stopping as necessary to scrape down sides of work bowl. Add vanilla, baking powder and salt and blend 30 seconds. (*Can be prepared ahead to this point and chilled.*)

Transfer sauce to top of double boiler set over simmering water. Warm until sugar is completely dissolved and sauce is heated through, stirring occasionally, about 15 minutes. Serve hot.

Burgundy Wine and Honey Sauce

A great basting glaze for baked ham.

Makes about 2 cups

1 cup dark corn syrup
1/2 cup honey
1 tablespoon grated lemon peel
1/4 teaspoon cinnamon

10 whole cloves
3/4 cup Burgundy or other dry red wine

Combine syrup and honey in heavy medium saucepan and bring to boil. Add peel, cinnamon and cloves. Remove from heat. Cover and cool completely. Stir in wine. Strain sauce. Store in airtight container.

Brandied Vanilla Essence

Whenever a recipe calls for vanilla, use this sweet-smelling flavoring instead. For best results, use top-quality brandy and moist and fragrant vanilla beans.

Makes 1 quart

8 vanilla beans
4 cups brandy

Additional vanilla beans (optional)

Cut 8 vanilla beans crosswise into thirds. Using very sharp knife, split each piece open lengthwise; do not cut through. Place pieces in jar. Cover with brandy. Seal tightly; shake well. Let stand 3 weeks at room temperature, shaking jar several times a week. Open jar; aroma should be very rich with vanilla. If not, let stand 1 more week. Strain essence through coffee filter paper. Using funnel, fill narrow-necked bottles with essence, leaving 1/4-inch space at top. Add 1 vanilla bean to each if desired. Seal tightly. Store in cool dark place.

Grandmother's Sauce

Package this sauce with homemade steamed pudding or gingerbread.

Makes about 4 cups

1 egg
1 cup sugar
1/4 cup melted butter

1 teaspoon vanilla
1 1/2 cups whipping cream, whipped

Beat egg in large bowl of electric mixer until thick and lemon colored. Gradually add sugar, beating until thickened, about 2 to 3 minutes. Stir in melted butter and vanilla using rubber spatula. Gently fold in whipped cream. Chill at least 1 hour.

🍎 *Flavored Oils, Vinegars and Mustards*

Basic Herb Vinegar

If using soft-stemmed annuals, the stem is used as well as the leaves. With the perennials, the woody stem should be reserved for use in stocks, or just discarded. It is most important that the fresh herbs fill exactly two thirds of the container being used.

Makes about 1 gallon

12 to 16 ounces fresh herbs, stemmed as necessary
3½ to 4 quarts (about) distilled white vinegar

Additional fresh herb branches

Wash herbs briefly under running water. Drain in colander 1 to 2 hours.

Add herbs to fill ²/₃ of 1-gallon container. Fill with vinegar, leaving ¼-inch head space. Cover tightly with plastic wrap or lid. Store mixture in cool place (55°F to 60°F) until flavor develops, 3 to 4 weeks.

Strain vinegar through fine sieve set over glass or ceramic large container. Let vinegar stand overnight.

Insert fresh herb branch into sterilized jars for garnish and identification. Carefully pour vinegar through funnel into jars, being careful not to disturb sediment in bottom of container. Cap or seal bottles. Store vinegar in cool dark area until ready to use.

Variations

Add these flavorings to the basic herb and vinegar mixture before allowing the flavors to develop.

Dill-Lemon-Fennel Seed Vinegar: Add 1 medium lemon (cut into 6 wedges) and 1 tablespoon cracked fennel seed to basic dill vinegar mixture.

Oregano-Garlic-Red Chili Vinegar: Add 8 ounces peeled garlic, 6 dried red chilies and 8 ounces oregano to 3½ quarts of distilled white vinegar.

Chive Vinegar: Mix 8 ounces chives with 3½ quarts vinegar.

Savory-Thyme Vinegar: Use ²/₃ summer savory and ¹/₃ thyme *or* ½ winter savory and ½ thyme as blend for basic herb vinegar mixture.

Fresh Basil Vinegar

An aromatic dressing for fresh tomatoes or over split sourdough rolls for pan bagnat, *the basis of a sandwich popular in the south of France.*

Makes 1 quart

1 cup (about) fresh basil sprigs
1 quart red wine vinegar

Place basil in tall 1-quart glass bottle. Pour vinegar over almost to fill. Cap and seal. Let stand in warm, sunny area for 10 days to 2 weeks to infuse.

Rosemary or Thyme Vinegar

Sharply pungent, palate-provoking vinegars to use in marinades for lamb or duck, or to dress meat salads or greens such as escarole and curly endive.

Makes 1 quart

4 or 5 whole black peppercorns
1 cup (about) fresh rosemary or thyme branches (or a combination)

1 quart red wine vinegar, room temperature

Place peppercorns and herbs in tall 1-quart glass bottle. Pour vinegar over almost to fill. Cap and seal. Let stand in warm, sunny area for 10 days to 2 weeks to infuse before using.

Hot Peppered Old South Vinegar

In the South, it's traditional to keep a cruet of this vinegar on the table to sprinkle over wilted or steamed greens.

Makes 1 quart

¹/₄ pound fresh green or red hot chili peppers

1 quart cider vinegar

Scald peppers in boiling water 60 seconds. Handling carefully, rinse under cold running water until cool. Place in 1-quart glass bottle or divide between two 1-pint glass cruets. Fill with vinegar. Cap and seal. Let stand in cool, dark area for 10 days to infuse.

Basic Fruit Vinegar

Fruit vinegars are divided into two main categories: berry vinegars and stone fruit vinegars. The only difference between the two is the method of preparing the fruit before crushing. This recipe can be doubled or tripled.

Makes about 4 to 5 cups

4 pounds fresh berries or red or black currants
   or
5 pounds stone fruits (such as peaches, damson plums or sour cherries)

1 quart distilled white vinegar

Sugar

Berry or stone fruit leaves (garnish)

Sort fruit, discarding leaves and any molded or bruised fruit; it is unnecessary to hull strawberries or to remove stalks from currants or tops and tails from gooseberries. Rinse fruit if necessary and drain in colander. Cut large varieties of stone fruits into ¹/₂-inch sections. Discard pits; peeling is unnecessary. It is not necessary to pit plums and sour cherries. Weigh fruit; you should have about 4 pounds. Transfer to 1-gallon glass or ceramic container. Using potato masher or hands, crush fruit to release juices.

Blend in vinegar. Cover tightly with plastic wrap or lid. Store in cool place (55°F to 60°F) until flavor develops, 3 to 4 weeks, stirring every other day.

Line large glass or ceramic bowl with pillowcase or sheet. Pour in fruit and vinegar. Gather up 4 corners of fabric and knot onto solid piece of wood (broomstick handle works well). Hang mixture up over bowl overnight to allow vinegar to drain into bowl; do not squeeze fruit mixture.

Preheat oven to 300°F. Discard drained fruit. Measure vinegar; measure 3 tablespoons sugar for every 2 cups vinegar. Place sugar in baking pan. Warm sugar in oven 8 to 10 minutes. Meanwhile, pour vinegar into large wide pot that is no more than 8 inches deep; vinegar should be no more than 4 inches deep. (*Cook vinegar in batches if proper pot is unavailable. Keeping vinegar shallow expedites boiling process, which preserves color of vinegar.*) Place vinegar over high heat and warm through. Stir in warmed sugar and quickly bring to boil. Boil 3 minutes to prevent fermentation. Pour into clean container. Let stand overnight before proceeding.

Add appropriate garnish to sterilized bottles. Slowly and carefully decant vinegar into bottles; discard sediment remaining in container. Cap or seal bottles. Store bottles of vinegar in cool dark area until ready to use.

Variations

Add these flavorings to the basic fruit and vinegar mixture before allowing the flavors to develop.

Peach-Ginger Vinegar: Add 2 ounces peeled ginger, cut into 1/4-inch slices, to basic peach vinegar mixture.

Blueberry-Mint Vinegar: Use only 3 pounds of berries for basic fruit vinegar. Add 2 ounces mint branches.

Cranberry Vinegar

Use this fragrant vinegar to deglaze or baste a holiday turkey, duck or ham or to dress a winter fruit salad. Combine with walnut or hazelnut oil for a delicate vinaigrette for hearty winter greens.

Makes about 1 quart

4 cups whole cranberries (1 pound), sorted
4 cups white wine vinegar

2/3 cup sugar
1 6-inch strip orange peel (orange part only)

Set aside 16 cranberries; coarsely chop remainder. Place in deep nonaluminum bowl. Bring vinegar just to simmer. Pour over chopped berries. Cover bowl with 3 layers of cheesecloth. Let stand in cool area 36 hours (do not refrigerate), stirring every 12 hours.

Strain vinegar through cheesecloth-lined sieve into deep nonaluminum saucepan, pressing to extract as much juice as possible. Mix in sugar. Stir over low heat until sugar dissolves, 3 to 4 minutes. Divide reserved whole berries among glass bottles. Cut orange peel into as many pieces as bottles and add 1 piece to each. Pour hot vinegar into hot bottles, leaving 1/2-inch space at top. Seal immediately. Store in cool dark place up to 3 months.

Rose Petal Vinegar

Use this delicately aromatic vinegar to dress salad greens, or use it to sprinkle over fresh berries or melon wedges.

Makes about 1 quart

1/2 cup fresh rose petals (pick in early morning when they still retain dew)

1 quart distilled white vinegar

Place rose petals in 1-quart glass jar or bottle. Bring vinegar to simmer, then pour over petals. Cap and seal. Let stand in warm, sunny area for about 1 week to infuse before using.

Ginger and Spice Vinegar

Use this special vinegar for English Pub-style Pickled Eggs (see page 41).

Makes about 1 quart

1 tablespoon coarse salt
2 1/4-inch-thick slices fresh ginger
2 teaspoons whole allspice berries
1 teaspoon whole black peppercorns

1 quart malt or cider vinegar
1/2 cup sugar

Place salt and seasoning in 1-quart glass bottle or jar. Combine vinegar and sugar in nonaluminum saucepan and bring to simmer. Pour into bottle to fill. Cap and seal. Let stand in cool dark area for 10 days to infuse before using.

Fresh Herb-Infused Oil

Use in salads, brush over fish and poultry for the grill, rub into meats and poultry before roasting, or offer a cruet at table to sprinkle over broiled meats.

For each jar:
Fresh herbs such as tarragon, thyme, mint and oregano

Olive oil

Half-fill a bottle or jar with a variety of herbs. Add olive oil almost to fill. Cap. Store in cool, dark area for 10 days to infuse before using.

Double Olive Oil

Cured olives enhance the flavor of olive oil. This is a gift to give with pride.

Makes 1 quart

1 cup oil-cured Italian or Greek olives

Olive oil

Place olives in 1-quart glass bottle. Add olive oil almost to fill. Cap. Store in cool, dark area for 10 days before using.

Olive Oil Flavored with Porcini Mushrooms, Garlic and Herbs

An ultrasimple recipe that takes only minutes to prepare. Best if allowed to mellow one month. Toss the oil with hot pasta or roasted potatoes. Once the oil is gone, sauté the porcini mushrooms and use in an omelet or salad.

Makes about 1 quart

1 ½ ounces large dried porcini mushrooms
16 whole black peppercorns
4 medium garlic cloves, slashed
4 4-inch fresh thyme sprigs

2 6-inch fresh rosemary sprigs
2 large bay leaves (preferably imported)
4 cups virgin olive oil (do not use extra-virgin)

Rinse mushrooms briefly under cold water. Shake dry. Dry completely on paper towels, about 1 hour.

Divide all ingredients except oil among bottles. Using funnel, pour oil into bottles, leaving ½-inch space at top. Seal bottles tightly. Let stand in cool dark place 4 weeks to mellow.

Dijon Mustard Vinaigrette

Makes about 2 cups

1 hard-cooked medium egg, chopped
1 medium egg yolk
3 tablespoons Dijon mustard
1 tablespoon minced onion
2 teaspoons minced shallot
2 teaspoons chopped fresh oregano
2 teaspoons (or more) chopped fresh parsley

1 garlic clove, minced
1 teaspoon chopped fresh basil
½ teaspoon salt
Pinch of sugar
Freshly ground pepper
3 tablespoons distilled white wine
3 tablespoons white wine vinegar
1 cup olive oil

Combine all ingredients except wine, vinegar and oil in medium bowl. Beat in wine and vinegar. Whisk in oil in slow steady stream. Cover vinaigrette and refrigerate until ready to use.

Poppy Seed Dressing

Perfect over a spinach salad studded with crumbled bacon and avocado.

Makes about 1 cup

1/4 cup white wine vinegar
4 teaspoons sugar
2/3 teaspoon dry mustard
2/3 teaspoon salt

2 teaspoons fresh lemon juice
2/3 cup vegetable oil
1 tablespoon poppy seed

Combine vinegar, sugar, mustard and salt in blender or processor and mix well. Add lemon juice. With machine running, gradually add oil. Stir in poppy seed. Store dressing in tightly covered jar in refrigerator.

Onion Salad Dressing

Makes about 1 cup

1/2 cup finely chopped onion
1/4 cup cider vinegar
1/4 cup sugar
1/2 teaspoon salt

1/2 teaspoon dry mustard
1/4 teaspoon celery seed
1/2 cup vegetable oil

Combine all ingredients except oil in blender and mix well, stopping as necessary to scrape down sides of container. With machine running, gradually pour in oil, blending until dressing is creamy. Transfer to container with tight fitting lid and refrigerate before using. Whisk or shake if dressing begins to separate on standing.

Polli's House Dressing

From Polli's On The Beach in Kihei, Maui. This creamy, sweet-tart dressing will make almost any salad special.

Makes 1 1/4 cups

1/2 cup vegetable oil
1/4 cup cashews
1/4 cup water
3 tablespoons honey
1 tablespoon fresh lemon juice

2 teaspoons distilled white vinegar
1 1/2 teaspoons dried dillweed
3/4 teaspoon light soy sauce
2 garlic cloves

Mix all ingredients in blender until very smooth. Store in jar in refrigerator.

Flavored Dijon Mustards

The following six recipes are especially quick and delicious. All use 1 cup of good quality prepared Dijon mustard as the base.

Makes about 1 cup

Moutarde aux Herbes de Provence

1 tablespoon mixed Herbes de Provence

1 tablespoon dry vermouth
1 cup prepared Dijon mustard

Combine Herbes de Provence and vermouth in small bowl and let stand about 20 minutes. Gradually whisk in mustard. Transfer to jar with tight-fitting lid. Store in cool, dark place.

Moutarde au Citron

Makes about 1 cup

1 cup prepared Dijon mustard
1 tablespoon fresh lemon juice

1 teaspoon honey
Grated peel of 1 lemon

Whisk all ingredients in medium bowl. Transfer to jar with tight-fitting lid. Store in cool, dark place.

Moutarde aux Echalotes

Makes about 1 cup

1 cup prepared Dijon mustard
2 tablespoons finely minced shallot

$\frac{1}{2}$ teaspoon dried chervil, crumbled

Combine all ingredients in medium bowl and whisk until well blended. Transfer to jar with tight-fitting lid. Store in cool, dark place.

Moutarde aux Olives Noires

Makes about $1\frac{1}{4}$ cups

$\frac{1}{4}$ cup pitted Greek or
Mediterranean olives

1 cup prepared Dijon mustard

Puree olives in processor until creamy. Add Dijon mustard and mix until well blended. Transfer to jar with tight-fitting lid. Store in cool, dark place.

Celery Mustard

Makes about $1\frac{1}{4}$ cups

$\frac{1}{4}$ cup celery leaves
1 teaspoon celery seed

1 cup prepared Dijon mustard

Combine celery leaves and celery seed in processor and mix until well blended. Add Dijon mustard and blend again. Transfer to jar with tight-fitting lid. Store in cool, dark place.

Lime Mustard

Makes about 1 cup

1 cup prepared Dijon mustard
1 tablespoon fresh lime juice

1 teaspoon honey
Finely grated peel of 1 lime

Whisk all ingredients in medium bowl. Transfer to jar with tight-fitting lid. Store in cool, dark place.

Green Chili Mustard with Green Peppercorns

Team this spicy condiment with a jar of Roasted Red Pepper Mustard (see recipe below) as a gift. Delicious with ham, roasted poultry and roasted veal sausages; a deluxe addition to sandwiches.

Makes about 2 cups

4 fresh Anaheim chilies
2 small jalapeño chilies

²/₃ cup imported English-style dry mustard
1 cup Sherry vinegar
1 cup boiling water

1 cup medium-dry Sherry
1 2-inch cinnamon stick
1 tablespoon coarse kosher salt

1 teaspoon cumin seed, coarsely crushed
1 teaspoon coriander seed, coarsely crushed
¹/₈ teaspoon ground cloves

1 tablespoon firmly packed light brown sugar
2 tablespoons green peppercorns
4 teaspoons green peppercorns

Char Anaheim and jalapeño chilies over gas flame or in broiler until blackened on all sides. Wrap in paper bag and let stand 10 minutes. Peel and seed. Rinse if necessary; pat dry. Cut Anaheim chilies into ¹/₄-inch dice. Cut jalapeños into ¹/₈-inch dice.

Place mustard in medium bowl. Add vinegar and boiling water, whisking until mixture is smooth. Cover and let mustard mellow for 3 hours.

Simmer Sherry, cinnamon, salt, cumin, coriander and cloves in heavy non-aluminum saucepan 7 minutes.

Strain Sherry mixture through fine sieve into mustard. Stir in sugar and 2 tablespoons peppercorns. Puree mixture in processor until smooth, using quick on/off turns and stopping to scrape down sides of work bowl. Return to saucepan. Set saucepan in larger pan of simmering water. Cook until mustard is consistency of mayonnaise, stirring frequently, 20 to 30 minutes. Mix in chilies and 4 teaspoons peppercorns. Pack into hot glass jars. Cool completely. Seal tightly and refrigerate mustard at least 1 week to mellow flavors. (*Can be stored in refrigerator 3 months.*)

Roasted Red Pepper Mustard

Great with grilled Italian sausages, roast pork or lamb sandwiches. Decorate jars with clusters of small dried red chili peppers and bay leaves.

Makes about 3 cups

1¹/₂ pounds red bell peppers
10 drops hot pepper sauce
¹/₄ teaspoon cayenne pepper

³/₄ cup imported English-style dry mustard
1¹/₄ cups boiling water
³/₄ cup red wine vinegar
¹/₂ cup Sherry vinegar
3 tablespoons mustard seed

²/₃ cup medium-dry Sherry
¹/₂ cup dry red wine

1 medium garlic clove, halved
1 tablespoon coarse kosher salt
1 teaspoon crushed black peppercorns
³/₄ teaspoon crushed whole allspice

2 tablespoons honey
1¹/₂ teaspoons dried thyme, crumbled
3 bay leaves
3 fresh thyme sprigs

Char bell peppers over gas flame or in broiler until blackened on all sides. Wrap in paper bag and let stand 10 minutes. Peel and seed. Rinse if necessary; pat dry. Puree in processor until smooth. Mix in hot pepper sauce and cayenne pepper. Transfer to bowl.

Place dry mustard in medium bowl. Add water, both vinegars and mustard seed, whisking until mustard is smooth. Cover and let mellow 2 hours.

Combine Sherry, wine, garlic, salt, black pepper and allspice in heavy non-aluminum saucepan. Cover partially and simmer 7 minutes.

Strain Sherry mixture through fine sieve into mustard. Stir in honey and dried thyme. Return to saucepan. Set saucepan in larger pan of simmering water. Cook until consistency of mayonnaise, stirring frequently, 20 to 30 minutes. Whisk in red pepper puree. Pack mustard into hot jars. Top each with bay leaf and thyme sprig. Cool completely. Seal tightly and refrigerate 1 week to mellow flavors. (*Can be stored in refrigerator 3 months.*)

Spicy Molasses Mustard

This hot mustard goes well with grilled sausages and cold meats.

Makes about 1 cup

1 cup dry mustard
6 tablespoons water or beer
6 tablespoons molasses
6 tablespoons apple cider vinegar

1/2 teaspoon *each* ground allspice, cinnamon, salt and freshly ground pepper
1/4 teaspoon ground cloves

Combine mustard and water or beer in stainless steel bowl and whisk until well blended. Let stand 15 minutes. Add remaining ingredients and blend well. Transfer to jar with tight-fitting lid. Store in cool, dark place.

 ### *Making Mustards to Give*

- Homemade mustards should be tightly sealed and stored in a cool, dark place. They will keep this way for months and will last indefinitely if stored in the refrigerator.

- English dry mustard has a fiery bite. French dry mustard is a milder version. Choose accordingly when planning your shopping list.

- Natural food stores and shops selling herbs and spices in bulk often have mustard in both dry powder and whole seed form. Look for both the yellow and black varieties of whole mustard seed. Each will impart its own character to the finished product.

- Small jars and bottles can be purchased from cookware shops, hardware stores and chemical supply houses. Or you can save your own interesting jars. Widemouthed bottles and jars with clamp-type tops are preferable: they allow you to reseal the mustard jar after each use, and are handsome to use as well as to give. Make sure that all jars are freshly washed and completely clean. Dry well before filling.

- For gift presentation, package individual jars in clear cellophane, tying with a festive grosgrain or silk ribbon. Add a tag with suggestions for using each mustard, and date it.

- Select attractive baskets and fill them with an assortment of small jars of homemade mustard. Add a hard salami, some cheeses and a loaf of crusty bread. Line the gift basket with natural raffia, and include a wooden paddle or two for serving the mustards.

- Present a cooking friend with an assortment of sausages, a homemade pâté, a loaf of hearty peasant bread, a jar or two of your own mustard and several bottles of assorted beers. Tie it all up in a festive tablecloth.

Monk-Style Black Mustard Seed Mustard

A coarse, grainy mustard that uses whole black mustard seed. Great with corned beef, boiled beef, pastrami or simmered country sausages.

Makes about 3 cups

1 cup whole black mustard seed
3/4 cup white wine vinegar
1/4 cup Sherry
2 cups dry mustard
3/4 cup firmly packed light brown sugar
1/2 teaspoon salt

Combine mustard seed, vinegar and Sherry in medium bowl and let stand 2 to 3 hours. Transfer mixture to processor and blend until almost smooth (mustard will be grainy). Add dry mustard, brown sugar and salt and blend well. Transfer to top of double boiler. Set over simmering water and cook 7 minutes, whisking constantly. Let cool. Transfer to jar with tight-fitting lid. Store mustard in cool, dark place.

English Pub Mustard

An easy-to-prepare mustard that is good with sausage, cold cuts, or as an accompaniment to an English plowman's lunch of cheese, bread, pickled onions and radishes.

Makes about 2 cups

2 cups dry mustard
1 cup firmly packed brown sugar
2 teaspoons salt
1/2 teaspoon turmeric
10 to 12 ounces flat beer or ale

Combine mustard, brown sugar, salt and turmeric in processor or blender and mix well. With machine running, add beer through feed tube in slow steady stream and blend until mixture is smooth and creamy, stopping frequently to scrape down sides of work bowl. Transfer to jar with tight-fitting lid. Store in cool, dark place.

 *Seasonings*

Garam Masala

A blending of roasted and ground spices that gives sparkle to cream-based sauces. Delicious rubbed into meats or poultry before grilling. Garam Masala can be frozen up to six months.

Makes about 1/2 cup

1 tablespoon whole cumin
1 tablespoon whole coriander
8 whole cloves
2 teaspoons whole cardamom seed (preferably green)
1 1/2 teaspoons peppercorns
4 dried red chilies* or 1/4 cup pure ground chili
1 teaspoon ground turmeric

Preheat oven to 300°F. Spread cumin, coriander, cloves, cardamom and peppercorns in shallow pan and roast 5 minutes. Add chilies and roast 2 more minutes. Remove from heat. Seed and devein chilies, if desired. Transfer spices and chilies to processor or blender. Add turmeric and mix to powder. Transfer to jar or bag, seal tightly and freeze.

*California chilies are mild, New Mexico "string" pods are hotter, ancho (pasilla) chilies still hotter and pequin or tepin chilies very hot. Choose according to your taste.

Sonoran Seasoning

*Excellent on grilled
seafood, meats, poultry
and vegetables.*

Makes about 1 cup

1 tablespoon pure chili powder

6 tablespoons plus 1½ teaspoons salt

4½ teaspoons black peppercorns

4 teaspoons cumin seed

4 teaspoons granulated garlic

1 tablespoon chamomile*

1 tablespoon granulated onion

1½ teaspoons paprika

¾ teaspoon white peppercorns

1 star anise point*

¼ teaspoon (scant) dried orange bits*

¼ teaspoon (scant) dried orange blossoms*

Pinch of cinnamon

Preheat oven to 250°F. Spread chili powder on small baking pan. Bake until beginning to darken, 5 to 7 minutes. Combine with all remaining ingredients in blender. Grind finely, about 1 minute. Store in jar.

*Available at specialty shops and natural food stores. If orange bits and dried orange blossoms are unavailable, substitute ¼ teaspoon orange spice tea.

Spicy Blend

*Substitute these next two
mixtures for salt on meats,
poultry, fish and salads.*

Makes about ⅓ cup

2 tablespoons dried savory, crumbled

1 tablespoon dry mustard

2½ teaspoons onion powder

1¾ teaspoons curry powder

1¼ teaspoons freshly ground white pepper

1¼ teaspoons ground cumin

½ teaspoon garlic powder

Combine all ingredients in small bowl and blend well. Spoon into shaker. Store in a cool dark place.

Herbed Seasoning

Makes about ⅓ cup

2 tablespoons dried dillweed or basil leaves, crumbled

2 tablespoons onion powder

1 teaspoon dried oregano leaves, crumbled

1 teaspoon celery seed

¼ teaspoon grated dried lemon peel

Pinch of freshly ground pepper

Combine all ingredients in small bowl and blend well. Spoon into shaker. Store in a cool dark place.

Curry Paste

This seasoning is delicious with grilled seafood.

Makes 1 cup

2 tablespoons ground turmeric
1 tablespoon ground coriander
1 tablespoon ground cumin
1 tablespoon ground aniseed
1½ teaspoons minced garlic
1½ teaspoons minced onion
1 teaspoon salt

¾ teaspoon cinnamon
¼ teaspoon ground cloves

½ cup vegetable oil
¼ cup vinegar
1 teaspoon cayenne pepper

Preheat oven to 150°F. Mix all dry ingredients except cayenne pepper in shallow baking pan. Bake 2 hours, shaking pan occasionally.

Whisk oil, vinegar and cayenne pepper into baking pan. Warm mixture over low heat to blend flavors, about 10 minutes. Cool mixture completely before using. Store in refrigerator.

4 ❦ *Pickles, Relishes and Chutneys*

Standard end-of-summer procedure in any country kitchen involves the bringing out of jars, kettles and other time-honored canning paraphernalia. Making pickles and relishes is a wonderfully satisfying process that celebrates a bountiful harvest—or, in cities, the welcome sight of farmer's markets overflowing with produce.

Pickles, relishes and chutneys are among the most traditional of food gifts. They keep on the shelf for a long time, they attest to the culinary skills of the giver, and for the recipient they bring sparkle to everyday foods. From simple Five-Day Pickles (page 38) to the more elaborate Turkish Stuffed Peppers (page 44), the recipes in this chapter represent an international array of homemade condiments.

Whatever the occasion, these gifts are right, whether it's Cranberry Chutney (page 46) to be served with turkey, or Pickled Ruby Eggs (page 41) to take along on a summer picnic. Eggplant Laura (page 42) makes a wonderful dinner party appetizer, and Double Pear and Walnut Mincemeat (page 49) a very inventive dessert pie filling (be sure to include a recipe for making the pie with this gift).

Mediterranean-Style Marinated Mushrooms

An appealing antipasto selection or appetizer. Wrap it up in a pretty jar with a loaf of crusty bread to absorb every last bit of savory sauce.

6 to 8 appetizer servings

Marinade
- 1/4 cup olive oil
- 8 coriander seeds
- 4 large shallots, minced
- 2 large garlic cloves, minced
- 1 large tomato, peeled, seeded and coarsely chopped
- 1 tablespoon tomato paste
- 1 tablespoon fresh lemon juice
- 1 teaspoon dried basil

- 1/2 teaspoon dried tarragon
- 1/2 teaspoon salt
  Freshly ground pepper
  Pinch of sugar

- 24 firm mushrooms (1 pound total), stems cut even with cap
- 1 cup Kalamata olives, drained
- 1/4 cup minced fresh parsley leaves

Combine all ingredients for marinade and blend well. Chill in airtight container 3 days, stirring occasionally.

Combine marinade with mushroom caps in large skillet. Place over medium-low heat and bring just to simmer, stirring frequently. Transfer to bowl and add olives. Let cool, then chill. Bring to room temperature before serving. Garnish with parsley. (*Marinated mushrooms can be refrigerated several days in airtight container.*)

Five-Day Pickles

These simple pickles are a snap to prepare and a favorite holiday gift.

Makes about 2 quarts

- 2 to 3 large cucumbers (unpeeled), thinly sliced
- 2 large onions, thinly sliced
- 2 cups sugar
- 2 cups white wine vinegar

- 3/4 teaspoon celery seed
- 3/4 teaspoon lemon pepper
- 3/4 teaspoon turmeric
- 3/4 teaspoon mustard seed
- 1/4 teaspoon salt

Layer cucumber and onion in sterilized jars, packing tightly. Combine remaining ingredients in medium saucepan over low heat and stir constantly until sugar is dissolved, about 10 minutes. Pour evenly into jars and seal. Let cool slightly. Refrigerate at least 5 days before serving.

Kosher Pickles

Makes 1 gallon

- 4 pounds pickling cucumbers, thoroughly washed
- 1/4 cup salt
- 8 cups water
- 5 garlic cloves, coarsely chopped

- 2 tablespoons mixed pickling spices
- 1 bunch fresh dill
- 1 slice day-old Jewish-style rye bread

Arrange cucumbers in 1-gallon glass jar or stoneware crock. Stir salt into water and pour into jar. Add garlic and pickling spices. Lay dill over top. Add rye bread. Cover with plastic wrap and weight with small heavy object to keep cucumbers submerged. Let stand at room temperature 3 days, then refrigerate at least 5 days before serving.

Pickled Onions

This recipe also includes an easy method for making spiced vinegar.

6 servings

1 quart malt vinegar
1 generous tablespoon white peppercorns
1 generous tablespoon ground ginger
1 generous tablespoon whole cloves

1 generous tablespoon allspice
1 generous tablespoon cinnamon

12 small yellow or boiling onions
2¼ cups water mixed with
1 teaspoon salt

Combine vinegar and spices in heatproof bowl and cover with plate. Set bowl in slightly larger saucepan of cold water and bring to boil over medium heat. Remove bowl from saucepan. Let stand at room temperature 2 hours; do not remove plate. Strain.

Peel and skin onions, placing in salted water as each is finished. Drain thoroughly. Pack onions into sterilized jar. Cover with vinegar. Seal and let stand at room temperature at least 1 month.

Peppers Preserved in Vinegar (Peperoni Sott' Aceto)

Excellent as part of an antipasto. The peppers can be sprinkled with olive oil and minced garlic if desired.

Makes about 1¾ pounds

4 1-inch pickling onions*
1¾ pounds red or combination of red and yellow bell peppers (ribs discarded), cut lengthwise into 1-inch strips
1 teaspoon salt

2 cups plus 2 tablespoons white wine vinegar
¾ cup water
1 oregano sprig or 2 teaspoons dried, crumbled

Make 3 slashes ⅓ inch deep in both ends of pickling onions. Place in 1½-quart jar. Add peppers and sprinkle with salt. Pour vinegar and water into jar, adding more water if necessary to cover peppers. Add oregano. Cover and marinate at room temperature 3 weeks before serving. (*Peppers can be stored at room temperature up to 3 months.*)

*If unavailable, quarter 1 small onion.

Chef Gaertner's Plums in Vinegar (Prunes au Vinaigre)

These sweet and sour plums are excellent with grilled meats and charcuterie. When firm dark cherries are in season, try using them instead. Make at least two weeks ahead for maximum flavor.

Makes 1 quart

2 pounds firm Italian prune plums
5 whole cloves
1 3-inch cinnamon stick

1 bay leaf
1 pound sugar
2 cups distilled white vinegar

Pierce each plum in 3 places with wooden or plastic toothpick; do not use metal. Combine plums, cloves, cinnamon stick and bay leaf in large nonaluminum bowl. Cook sugar and vinegar in heavy large saucepan over low heat until sugar dissolves, swirling pan occasionally. Increase heat and bring to boil. Immediately pour over plums. Cool completely. Cover and let stand at room temperature 2 days.

Drain plums, reserving syrup. Bring syrup to boil. Pour over plums. Cool completely. Cover and let stand at room temperature 1 day.

Bring plums and syrup to boil in heavy large saucepan. Reduce heat and simmer 10 minutes. Drain, reserving syrup. Pack plums into sterilized 1½-quart jar. Boil syrup until reduced to 2 cups. Pour over plums and seal immediately (there may be some leftover syrup). Let plums stand at room temperature at least 2 weeks before using.

Sweet Yellow Squash Pickles

Blanch the onions about 30 seconds in boiling water, then peel. The skins will slip off—without tears.

Makes 6 to 8 pints

3 dozen boiling onions, peeled and thinly sliced
12 medium straight-neck yellow squash, thinly sliced
½ cup pickling or noniodized salt
1½ quarts cracked ice

1 quart distilled white vinegar
3½ cups sugar
1¾ teaspoons turmeric
1¾ teaspoons celery seed
1¾ teaspoons mustard seed

Layer onion and squash in large bowl, sprinkling each layer with pickling salt. Top with cracked ice. Let stand, uncovered, at room temperature 3 hours. Drain liquid. Turn vegetable mixture into colander and rinse well under cold running water. Drain; press out as much liquid as possible.

Combine vinegar, sugar, turmeric, celery seed and mustard seed in heavy large nonaluminum saucepan and bring to boil over high heat. Stir in onion and squash and return brine to boil. Remove from heat. Using slotted spoon, pack mixture into clean hot jars to ¼ inch from top, then cover vegetables with brine. Run thin-bladed knife around inside of jars to release any trapped air bubbles. Clean rims and threads of jars with damp cloth. Seal with new, scalded, very hot lids. Transfer jars to gently simmering water bath (180°F to 185°F) and process 10 minutes. Cool to room temperature; check seals. Store in cool dark place up to 1 year. Refrigerate after opening.

Italian Pickled Vegetables (Giardiniera)

Makes 8 quarts

2 pounds zucchini, cut into ¼ × 2½-inch julienne (do not peel)
2 bunches carrots, peeled and cut into ¼ × 2½-inch julienne
1 large cauliflower, cut into small florets
1 bunch broccoli florets
1 small bunch celery, cut into 1 × 3-inch strips
3 green bell peppers, cored, seeded and cut into ½-inch julienne
3 red bell peppers, cored, seeded and cut into ½-inch julienne
2 quarts water
2 cups coarse salt

4 quarts distilled white vinegar
3 cups sugar

½ cup mustard seed
½ cup celery seed
3 tablespoons ground turmeric
2 tablespoons black peppercorns
1 16-ounce jar red and green cherry peppers, well drained
1 14-ounce can pitted black olives, well drained
1 10-ounce jar pimiento-stuffed green olives, well drained
1 10-ounce jar peperoncini,* well drained
8 bay leaves
8 large garlic cloves
8 tiny dried red chilies

Combine zucchini, carrots, cauliflower, broccoli, celery and bell peppers in 1 or 2 large bowls. Bring water to boil in medium saucepan. Add salt and stir until dissolved. Let cool. Pour cooled brine evenly over vegetables, covering completely. Let stand for at least 8 hours, preferably overnight.

Drain vegetables and rinse thoroughly in cold water. Drain well. Combine vinegar, sugar, mustard seed, celery seed, turmeric and peppercorns in stockpot and bring to rapid boil over high heat. Stir in vegetables. Add cherry peppers, black olives, green olives and peperoncini and simmer 2 minutes. Remove from heat. Using slotted spoon, pack some of vegetables into 1 clean, hot quart jar to

½ inch from top. Add 1 bay leaf, 1 garlic clove and 1 chili to jar. Ladle enough brine over mixture just to cover. Run plastic knife or spatula between vegetables and jar to release any air bubbles. Clean rim and threads of jar with damp cloth. Seal with new, scalded, very hot lids. Repeat with remaining vegetable mixture. Transfer jars to gently simmering (180°F to 190°F) water bath and process for 20 minutes. Let jars cool on rack. Test for seal. Store vegetables in cool dry place.

For vegetable variation, substitute or add trimmed tiny artichokes (parboiled for 2 minutes), tiny whole onions, fresh fennel strips, baby turnips and brussels sprouts. Adjust bay leaves, dried red chilies and garlic cloves if desired.

* Available at Italian food markets.

English Pub-Style Pickled Eggs

Serve with coarse whole wheat bread, unsalted butter, thinly sliced ham, cheddar cheese and beer.

Makes 1 quart

12 hard-cooked eggs, shelled
1½ cups Ginger and Spice Vinegar (see recipe page 28)
6 whole allspice berries

2 bay leaves
1 teaspoon whole black peppercorns

Pack eggs into 1-quart widemouthed jar. Bring vinegar to boil in nonaluminum saucepan and let boil about 10 minutes. Add remaining ingredients to jar and ladle hot vinegar over eggs. Cap tightly. Let cool, then refrigerate at least 3 days before serving. (*Can be refrigerated up to 2 weeks.*)

Pickled Ruby Eggs

½ pound small fresh beets, trimmed
1 small onion, thinly sliced

¼ cup cider vinegar
2 tablespoons sugar
1 tablespoon chopped fresh mixed herbs (any combination of dill, thyme, oregano, basil) or 1 teaspoon dried, crumbled

4 hard-cooked eggs

Lettuce leaves
Salt and freshly ground pepper

Boil beets and onion in enough water to cover until beets are tender when pierced with knife, about 30 minutes (time will vary depending on size of beets). Let beets and onion cool in liquid. Drain, reserving 1½ cups liquid. Slice beets; set aside with onion.

Cook beet liquid, vinegar, sugar and herbs in heavy small saucepan over low heat until sugar dissolves, swirling pan occasionally. Increase heat and bring to boil. Add beets and onion; boil 5 minutes. Drain, reserving liquid.

Arrange eggs in widemouth canning jar. Place beets and onion atop eggs. Pour beet liquid over. Cover jar tightly. Refrigerate at least 12 hours.

To serve, line plates with lettuce. Cut eggs in half. Arrange halves cut side up on plates. Garnish with beets and onion. Sprinkle with salt and pepper. (*Pickled eggs can be prepared 1 week ahead and refrigerated.*)

Eggplant Laura

Prepare this intriguing appetizer two days ahead for maximum flavor.

8 to 10 servings

1 cup (or more) olive oil
2 large eggplants, peeled, halved lengthwise and sliced 1/8 inch thick
6 garlic cloves, sliced
1/2 large bunch basil, coarsely chopped (about 1/2 cup)

2 tablespoons red wine vinegar
Salt

Basil leaves

Heat 1 cup oil in heavy large skillet over medium-high heat. Cook eggplant in batches until crisp-tender (do not brown), adding more oil as necessary, about 2 minutes; do not turn. Remove using slotted spatula and drain on paper towels. Layer eggplant, garlic and chopped basil in large baking dish, sprinkling with vinegar and salt between layers. Cover and refrigerate for 2 days.

To serve, transfer to platter with slotted spoon. Garnish with basil leaves. Serve at room temperature.

Potato Caponata

8 to 10 servings

4 pounds boiling potatoes
Olive oil
2 teaspoons salt
2 large onions, coarsely chopped
1 large celery heart, diced
1 cup red wine vinegar

1 1/2 tablespoons sugar
1 1/2 cups Quick Tomato Sauce*
1/2 cup green olives, pitted and coarsely chopped
1/2 cup capers, drained and rinsed

Peel and dice potatoes. Cover with cold water and soak 5 minutes. Drain, rinse and drain again.

Heat 1 inch olive oil in heavy large skillet over medium-low heat. Add potatoes in batches (do not crowd) and cook 5 minutes. Increase heat to high and fry until golden brown, turning occasionally, about 8 minutes. Remove using slotted spoon and drain on paper towels. Sprinkle with salt. Pour off all but 1 cup oil from skillet. Add onions and celery and cook over medium-low heat until softened, stirring occasionally, about 10 minutes. Add vinegar and sugar and stir 2 minutes. Stir in potatoes and remaining ingredients. Serve at room temperature. (*Can be prepared 3 days ahead and refrigerated.*)

*Quick Tomato Sauce

Makes about 1 1/2 cups

1/4 cup olive oil
1/2 small onion, minced
2 garlic cloves, unpeeled, lightly crushed
3 cups drained canned tomatoes, seeded and chopped

2 tablespoons minced fresh parsley
2 tablespoons minced fresh basil
1 teaspoon salt
1 to 2 teaspoons honey

Heat oil in heavy medium skillet over medium-high heat. Add onion and garlic and stir until aromatic, about 3 minutes. Discard garlic. Stir in tomatoes, parsley, basil, salt and 1 teaspoon honey. Cover partially and boil until almost all liquid evaporates, about 15 minutes. Add remaining honey if desired. (*Can be prepared 3 days ahead. Cool completely, cover and refrigerate. Bring to room temperature before using.*)

Sun-Dried Italian Tomatoes in Flavored Oils

To ensure the characteristic full flavor and unique texture, these homestyle Italian tomatoes should sit in flavored oil four to eight weeks. They will keep indefinitely in airtight jars.

Makes 2 to 3 pints

6 pounds ripe Italian plum
  tomatoes
2 tablespoons salt

Flavorings (see Variations)
2¹/₂ to 3 cups oil (see Variations)

Preheat oven to 200°F. Line baking sheets with racks. Slice tomatoes open lengthwise but not completely in half (to resemble books). Arrange on racks cut side up. Sprinkle with salt. Bake until tomatoes reduce about 75 percent in size and weight, appear shriveled and deep red, and feel warm and dry (do not let harden), 7 to 9 hours.

Remove tomatoes from oven and cool 1 hour. Pack in pint jars (about 14 tomatoes per pint). Add choice of flavorings. Cover completely with oil. Seal jars tightly. Store at room temperature 4 to 8 weeks.

Variations

Rosemary-garlic: Add three 3-inch rosemary sprigs and 2 unpeeled slashed garlic cloves. Cover with olive oil.

Thyme: Add five 4-inch fresh thyme sprigs. Cover with olive oil.

Pepper-oregano: Add 16 black peppercorns, 8 coriander seeds and three 3-inch oregano sprigs. Top with olive oil.

Chinese style: Add 2 small dried red chiles. Cover with seasame oil or mixture of sesame oil and vegetable oil.

New Mexico Green Chili Condiment

Use as a sauce, blend into omelets or crepe fillings or add as a flavoring for soups, stews and casseroles.

Makes 2 cups

12 mild to hot green chilies, rinsed
  and dried, roasted, peeled, seeded

1 small garlic clove, minced

1 teaspoon minced onion
Salt

Preheat broiler. Pierce each pepper near stem with sharp, thin knife. Arrange peppers on broiler pan and roast on all sides until blistered (but not charred). Transfer to plastic or paper bag, close tightly and steam 15 minutes. Slip off skins; discard stems and seeds. Chop finely.

Combine chilies, garlic and onion in jar with tight-fitting lid. Add salt to taste and shake well. (*Green Chili Condiment can be refrigerated for several days or frozen for several months.*)

Jerusalem Artichoke Relish

Makes about 2 quarts

2 quarts water
1 cup salt
1¹/₂ pounds Jerusalem artichokes
3¹/₂ cups plus 2 tablespoons sugar
6 tablespoons all purpose flour
1¹/₂ tablespoons mustard seeds
1¹/₂ teaspoons freshly ground pepper

1¹/₂ teaspoons turmeric
1 quart distilled white vinegar
1¹/₂ pounds cabbage, finely chopped
2¹/₂ large green bell peppers, finely
  chopped
2 cups finely chopped onion

Mix water and salt in large bowl until salt dissolves. Cut Jerusalem artichokes into ¹/₈-inch-thick slices and add to water. Soak overnight.

Combine sugar, flour, mustard seeds, pepper and turmeric in heavy non-aluminum saucepan. Slowly mix in vinegar. Cook over low heat, stirring occasionally, until sugar dissolves. Increase heat and boil 3 minutes, stirring occasionally. Mix in cabbage, green peppers and onion. Simmer until crisp-tender, about 8 minutes. Drain artichokes and add to saucepan. Stir until heated through. Spoon mixture into sterilized jars. Cover tightly. Cool completely before serving. (*Can be stored in refrigerator 2 months.*)

Red Pepper Relish

Makes 3 pints

6 cups ½-inch pieces red bell pepper
4 cups finely chopped onion
8 garlic cloves, finely minced
3 to 4 serrano or jalapeño chilies, finely minced
3 tablespoons coarse salt

1¾ to 2¼ cups sugar*
1¾ cups cider vinegar
1 tablespoon mustard seed
1 tablespoon oregano
1 bay leaf

Mix red pepper, onion, garlic, chilies and salt in large bowl. Let stand 3 hours. Drain thoroughly (do not rinse). Combine remaining ingredients in large saucepan and bring to boil over medium-high heat. Let boil 10 minutes. Reduce heat to medium, stir in pepper mixture and cook until peppers are translucent but still slightly crunchy, about 30 to 45 minutes.

Pour relish into 1 clean, hot pint jar to ½ inch from top. Run plastic knife or spatula between relish and jar to release any air bubbles. Clean rim and threads of jar with damp cloth. Seal with new, scalded, very hot lid. Repeat with remaining jars. Transfer to gently simmering (180°F to 190°F) water bath and process for 15 minutes. Let jars cool on rack. Test for seal. Store in cool dry place.

*Amount of sugar can be adjusted to taste: Use 2¼ cups for sweet relish; 1¾ cups for tangy. For a tarter version, use only 1 cup.

Turkish Stuffed Peppers

Makes 4 quarts

5 pounds very small green and red bell peppers (about 5 to 6 per pound)
4 quarts water
1 cup salt

4 pounds green cabbage
1½ pounds onion
1½ cups coarsely chopped celery
2 large carrots
½ cup fresh parsley
6 to 8 garlic cloves
1 quart water
2 cups distilled white vinegar
½ cup sugar
2 tablespoons coarse salt
1 teaspoon celery seed
½ teaspoon mustard seed

4 bay leaves
6 cups water or 4 cups water and 2 cups olive oil
2 cups distilled white vinegar
3 tablespoons coarse salt
1 tablespoon black peppercorns
2 teaspoons turmeric
1 teaspoon coriander seed
1 teaspoon cumin
1 teaspoon mustard seed
1 teaspoon paprika
¼ to ½ teaspoon dried red pepper flakes

Cut crown off bell peppers ³/₄ inch from top. Remove and discard stems, seeds and pith; reserve caps. Blend water and salt in nonmetal bowl. Add peppers and caps. Refrigerate mixture for at least 8 hours or overnight.

Drain peppers and rinse under cold water. Drain well. Finely chop cabbage, onion, celery, carrots, parsley and garlic in batches in processor using on/off turns. Transfer cabbage mixture to stockpot. Add water, vinegar, sugar, salt, celery seed and mustard seed. Place over high heat and bring to boil. Reduce heat and simmer 20 minutes.

Drain cabbage mixture well. Spoon into peppers; replace caps. Divide peppers among 4 clean, hot quart jars. Add 1 bay leaf to each jar. Combine remaining ingredients in stockpot and bring to rapid boil over high heat. Let boil 3 minutes. Ladle enough hot brine into 1 jar just to cover peppers. Run plastic knife or spatula between peppers and jar to release any air bubbles. Clean rim and threads of jar with damp cloth. Seal with new, scalded, very hot lid. Repeat with remaining jars. Transfer jars to gently simmering (180°F to 190°F) water bath and process for 30 minutes. Let jars cool on rack. Test for seal. Store in cool dry place, inverting jars occasionally to prevent separation if using olive oil.

Marinated Greek Olives

Makes 1 pound

³/₄ cup fresh lime juice
³/₄ cup orange juice
¹/₃ cup water
3 garlic cloves, halved
1¹/₂ to 2 tablespoons fennel seed

Peels of 1 lime and 1 orange, cut into thin strips
1 pound ripe olives, drained

Avocado slices (garnish)

Combine first 6 ingredients in 1-quart jar with tight-fitting lid. Taste olives. If very salty, soak in cold water 1 hour and drain. Add olives to marinade and stir to blend well. Cover jar with plastic wrap and lid. Chill at least 24 hours.

To serve, drain olives, arrange on platter and garnish with avocado slices.

Piquant Olives

This will keep for a month in the refrigerator. Excellent with cocktails.

12 to 16 buffet servings

1 11-ounce jar Greek olives, undrained
1 cup light olive oil
Juice and peel of one large orange
3 tablespoons wine vinegar

6 garlic cloves, lightly crushed
2 dried hot red peppers, broken, or 1 tablespoon hot red pepper flakes
6 whole cloves

Combine all ingredients. Cover and refrigerate at least 4 days, stirring daily. Drain, discarding peel, garlic, peppers and cloves. Serve in shallow bowl.

Tomato Macadamia Nut Chutney

Makes about 3 cups

3 cups chopped peeled Italian plum tomatoes or one 35-ounce can peeled Italian plum tomatoes, undrained
1½ cups sugar
1 cup red wine vinegar
¼ cup Sherry vinegar
2 tablespoons minced fresh basil
6 garlic cloves, minced
2 teaspoons salt
Pinch of dried red pepper flakes
1 cup macadamia nuts
½ cup dried currants

Bring first 8 ingredients to boil in heavy large nonaluminum saucepan. Reduce heat and simmer briskly until thickened and reduced to 3 cups, stirring occasionally, about 2 hours. Stir in nuts and currants and simmer 5 minutes. Serve hot or cold. (*Can be stored several weeks in refrigerator.*)

Apple, Apricot and Walnut Chutney

For maximum flavor, prepare this condiment several days ahead.

Makes 3 pints

2 pounds tart green apples, peeled, cored and cut into ½-inch dice
1 pound dried apricot halves, halved
2 large onions, diced
2 cups apple cider vinegar
1 cup raisins
1 cup firmly packed light brown sugar
½ cup crystallized ginger, coarsely chopped
1 tablespoon whole mustard seed
½ teaspoon coarse kosher salt
½ teaspoon cayenne pepper
½ teaspoon coarsely cracked black peppercorns
½ teaspoon ground mace
¼ teaspoon ground cloves
2 4-inch cinnamon sticks
1¼ cups walnut pieces, toasted

Combine all ingredients except walnuts in heavy large nonaluminum pot and bring to boil. Reduce heat, cover partially and simmer gently until mixture is thick, stirring occasionally, 1 to 1½ hours. Uncover and simmer until mixture is consistency of preserves, stirring frequently, about 15 minutes. Stir in walnuts and simmer 5 minutes. Ladle into hot jars, leaving ½-inch space at top. Seal jars; cool completely. Refrigerate until ready to use.

Cranberry Chutney

Makes about 3½ cups

2 garlic cloves
1 onion, quartered
4 cups cranberries
1 cup golden raisins
½ cup firmly packed light brown sugar
⅓ cup cider vinegar
1 tablespoon mustard seed
¼ teaspoon dry mustard
¼ teaspoon ground ginger
¼ teaspoon ground allspice
¼ teaspoon ground cardamom
¼ teaspoon ground cloves
¼ teaspoon dried red pepper flakes

1 large pear, peeled, quartered and cored
¼ cup firmly packed light brown sugar

With machine running, drop garlic through processor feed tube and mince finely. Add onion and chop coarsely, using on/off turns. Transfer mixture to heavy

2-quart nonaluminum saucepan. Add remaining ingredients except pear and ¼ cup sugar. Bring to boil. Reduce heat and simmer until chutney is very thick, stirring frequently, about 40 minutes.

Coarsely chop pear in processor, using on/off turns. Add to chutney. Cook 10 more minutes, stirring frequently. Remove from heat and stir in ¼ cup light brown sugar. Serve warm. (*Can be refrigerated up to 4 weeks.*)

Lemon-Fig Chutney

Surprise a friend with this Greek-inspired chutney, a round of Greek bread, wedge of sharp cheese and small bottle of ouzo or retsina. Serve with roasted leg of lamb, poultry or ham.

Makes about 4 cups

2 medium lemons, peels removed with vegetable peeler (yellow part only)
1 pound dried figs, cut into ½-inch cubes
2 cups ½-inch dice unpeeled tart green apples
1 medium onion, cut into ¼-inch cubes
½ cup ¼-inch-dice candied citron
⅓ cup dried currants
⅓ cup golden raisins

2 cups sugar
½ cup dry white wine or dry vermouth
½ cup (or more) water
⅓ cup honey
12 whole cloves
1 4-inch cinnamon stick
⅓ cup toasted pine nuts
⅓ cup anise liqueur (such as ouzo, Pernod or Ricard)

Cut lemon peel into fine julienne. Remove all white pith from lemons. Cut lemons into ½-inch dice, discarding seeds. Combine peel and lemon dice in large bowl with figs, apples, onion, candied citron, currants and raisins.

Combine sugar, wine, ½ cup water, honey, cloves and cinnamon in heavy nonaluminum saucepan. Cook over low heat, swirling pan occasionally, until sugar dissolves. Add fig mixture. Increase heat and simmer until mixture begins to mound on spoon, stirring frequently and adding more water if mixture thickens before figs are plump, 1½ to 2 hours. Mix in pine nuts and liqueur. Simmer 5 minutes to blend flavors. Ladle hot chutney into hot jars, leaving ½-inch space at top. Cool completely. Seal jars. (*Refrigerate up to 3 months.*)

Quick Mango Chutney

Serve this chutney hot over a round of Brie.

Makes 4½ cups

1½ cups cider vinegar
1¼ cups sugar
1¼ cups firmly packed dark brown sugar
3 cups peeled and coarsely chopped mangoes, papayas or peaches
½ cup golden raisins
1 tablespoon fresh lemon juice
1 teaspoon minced fresh ginger
1 teaspoon cinnamon
1 teaspoon salt

1 teaspoon mustard seed or dry mustard
½ teaspoon minced garlic
½ teaspoon ground red pepper

Bring vinegar and sugars to boil in 5-quart saucepan over high heat. Reduce heat to medium-low and add remaining ingredients. Simmer until mixture thickens slightly, 20 to 25 minutes. Cool; chutney will continue to thicken. Store in sterilized jars in refrigerator.

Pineapple-Papaya Chutney

Any fruit that is not fully ripened, such as peaches, apricots, plums, mangoes or apples, can be substituted for either the pineapple and/or the papaya.

Makes 4 cups

3 cups pineapple chunks ($\frac{1}{2}$-inch chunks)
1$\frac{1}{4}$ cups distilled white vinegar
1 cup firmly packed brown sugar
1 medium onion, finely chopped
2 hot green peppers, finely chopped
2 garlic cloves, minced or pressed
$\frac{1}{2}$ cup chopped preserved ginger
$\frac{1}{2}$ cup seedless raisins
$\frac{1}{2}$ cup chopped papaya

$\frac{1}{2}$ fresh lime, peeled, seeded and chopped
$\frac{1}{4}$ cup chopped pitted dates
1 teaspoon cinnamon
$\frac{1}{2}$ teaspoon salt
$\frac{1}{4}$ teaspoon ground cloves
$\frac{1}{4}$ teaspoon ground allspice
$\frac{1}{4}$ teaspoon ground red pepper
$\frac{1}{4}$ cup fresh lemon juice

Combine all ingredients except lemon juice in heavy large saucepan and bring to boil. Reduce heat and simmer 1 hour, stirring frequently. Stir in lemon juice and simmer an additional 5 minutes. Cool completely before serving.

Tomato Conserve

Makes about 2 cups

2$\frac{1}{2}$ pounds fresh Italian plum tomatoes, peeled, seeded and coarsely chopped (reserve juice) or one 28-ounce can Italian plum tomatoes, undrained
1$\frac{1}{4}$ cups red or white wine vinegar

1 cup sugar
1 teaspoon salt
$\frac{1}{4}$ teaspoon ground red pepper
2 tablespoons minced garlic
2 tablespoons minced fresh ginger
2 tablespoons raisins

Bring tomatoes (and juice), vinegar, sugar, salt and ground red pepper to boil in heavy saucepan. Stir in garlic and ginger. Reduce heat, cover partially and simmer gently 1$\frac{1}{2}$ hours, stirring occasionally. Uncover and continue simmering, stirring frequently, until mixture mounds slightly on spoon, about 20 minutes. Cool. Stir in raisins. Adjust seasoning. Serve at room temperature. (*Can be stored several weeks in refrigerator.*)

Spicy Apple Catsup

This condiment teams well with sausages, roast pork and poultry.

Makes about 1 quart

6 pounds firm tart apples (such as McIntosh or winesap), peeled, cored and cut into 6 pieces each
2 cups diced onion
1 cup sugar
$\frac{1}{3}$ cup $\frac{1}{4}$-inch-dice crystallized ginger

1 tablespoon salt
2 teaspoons cinnamon
1 teaspoon freshly ground pepper
1 teaspoon ground cloves
1 teaspoon dry mustard
2 cups cider vinegar

Place apples in heavy nonaluminum saucepan. Add enough water to just cover. Bring to simmer over medium heat. Cook until apples are very soft and most of water evaporates, 45 to 60 minutes (depending on variety of apple used). Press mixture through food mill or sieve. Return to same pan.

Whisk all remaining ingredients into apples except vinegar. Stir in vinegar. Bring mixture to simmer. Reduce heat to low and simmer until consistency of thick applesauce, stirring frequently, about 1 hour. Ladle catsup into glass jars. Cool to room temperature. Cover tightly and refrigerate at least 24 hours before serving. (*Catsup can be stored in refrigerator for up to 3 months.*)

Walnut-Plum Catsup

A colorful English condiment.

Makes 2 quarts

5 pounds ripe red or purple plums
4 cups sugar

2 cups cider vinegar
1 teaspoon cinnamon
1/2 teaspoon freshly grated nutmeg or ground mace
1/4 teaspoon ground cloves

1 cup walnuts, toasted and finely chopped

Cook plums and sugar in heavy large nonaluminum stockpot over medium heat until mixture just simmers; if plums are not juicy, mash slightly with spoon to break skins and release enough juices to mix with sugar. Reduce heat to low, cover and simmer until plums are tender, stirring occasionally, about 30 minutes. Mash plums slightly with back of spoon and cook uncovered 10 minutes.

Strain mixture through fine sieve into very large bowl, pressing to release liquid and most of pulp. Transfer back to original stockpot. Discard skins and pits remaining in sieve.

To flavor vinegar, barely simmer vinegar and spices in nonaluminum medium saucepan 5 minutes. Stir into plum mixture. Cook over medium heat until reduced to about 2 quarts, stirring occasionally, about 30 minutes.

Remove from heat and stir in walnuts. Ladle into clean, tall, glass bottles or jars, using funnel as aid if necessary. Cool completely. Cap tightly and refrigerate until ready to use.

Double Pear and Walnut Mincemeat

Prepare at least five days ahead to let flavors mellow. Place a small jar in the center of a gift basket with pear brandy, assorted nuts in the shell and some ripe pears. Include a note suggesting using the mincemeat to fill tarts, cookies or baked apples or serving warm over rich vanilla ice cream.

Makes about 3 quarts

3 1/2 pounds firm Bartlett or Anjou pears, peeled, cored and cut into 1/2-inch dice
2 cups 1/4-inch-dice dried pears
2 cups pear nectar
1 medium-size green apple, peeled, cored and cut into 1/2-inch dice
1 cup firmly packed light brown sugar
3/4 cup fresh orange juice
2/3 cup fresh lemon juice
2/3 cup dried currants
2/3 cup raisins
2/3 cup 1/4-inch-dice candied citron
1/2 cup coarsely chopped crystallized ginger

2 tablespoons coarsely grated lemon peel
2 tablespoons coarsely grated orange peel
1 1/2 teaspoons cinnamon
1 teaspoon freshly grated nutmeg
1/2 teaspoon mace
1/2 teaspoon ground ginger
1/2 teaspoon ground allspice
1/2 teaspoon coarsely ground pepper
1/2 teaspoon salt

1 cup coarsely chopped toasted walnuts
1/2 cup pear brandy

Bring all ingredients except walnuts and brandy to boil in heavy nonaluminum saucepan, stirring constantly. Reduce heat to low. Cover partially and cook for 1 1/2 hours, stirring pear mixture occasionally.

Uncover pan and continue cooking until mincemeat is thickened to consistency of preserves, stirring frequently, about 45 minutes. Add walnuts and brandy. Cook until rethickened, stirring frequently, about 10 minutes. Spoon hot mincemeat into hot jars, leaving ½-inch space at top. Seal jars. Cool mincemeat completely. Refrigerate at least 5 days before using. (*Can be stored in refrigerator up to 3 months.*)

Mincemeat

For fullest flavor, mincemeat should be made at least 1 month before using. It keeps almost indefinitely, so if you have a batch that has become a little dry, simply stir in some brandy to moisten.

Makes about 12 cups

3 cups peeled grated tart apple
1²/₃ cups mixed chopped candied fruit peel
1²/₃ cups chopped dried apricots
1²/₃ cups currants
1²/₃ cups golden raisins
1¹/₃ cups dark raisins
1¹/₃ cups firmly packed dark brown sugar
8 ounces (about 4 cups) fresh white breadcrumbs

½ cup brandy
¹/₃ cup chopped blanched almonds
¹/₄ cup chopped preserved ginger
1 teaspoon ground allspice
1 teaspoon ground ginger
1 teaspoon cinnamon
1 teaspoon freshly grated nutmeg
Peel and juice of 2 lemons
Peel and juice of 1 orange

Prepare jars. Combine all ingredients in large mixing bowl and blend thoroughly. Pack into hot sterilized jars to within ½ inch of top and seal. Process 25 minutes in boiling water bath. Remove from water and let cool. Test for seal. Store in cool dark place.

Brandied fruits offer a delicious bonus—the liquid used for preserving is an excellent after-dinner liqueur in its own right. All these fruits need at least three months' standing time before serving, although if you can wait six months, that's even better! Ideally, the fruit should remain completely covered with liquid after processing in the boiling water bath, but some liquid loss occurs occasionally. This will not cause spoilage, but if you open the jars to add more liquid, the fruit must be reprocessed.

5 🍎 Jams and Preserves

Jams, jellies and preserves are almost symbolic of homey goodness—and the recipes cooks seem to turn to first when creating food gifts. Foremost in our cultural memory, if not in our actual childhood remembrances, is a vision of a motherly figure patiently stirring away at a jam pot, while warm, nurturing things such as apple pie and muffins bake in the oven.

With a nod at tradition, we offer here recipes for old favorites such as Red Pepper Jelly (page 52) and Spiked Fruit Compote (page 60), as well as more unusual variations like Viennese Beet Preserves (page 56) and Gingered Cranberry-Grapefruit Marmalade (page 55). There are also recipes from today's kitchens—such as Marvelous Microwave Marmalade (page 53), which is ready in minutes.

When packaging jams and preserves for giving, select beautifully shaped clear glass containers that will show off the jewel-like colors of something like Amber Clove Citrus Marmalade (page 54). Or give a ceramic tub of Prune-Port Butter (page 58) along with a fresh loaf of Honey Cake (see Chapter 6, page 84).

Apple Pepper Jelly

This makes a tasty accompaniment to roasts, cold meats or cream cheese.

Makes about 5 cups

2 pounds Granny Smith apples, quartered (do not peel or core)
1½ cups water

2 green bell peppers, seeded and cut into 1-inch pieces
6 jalapeño chilies, seeded and cut into 1-inch pieces

5 cups sugar
1 cup cider vinegar
3 ounces liquid pectin
2 tablespoons minced red bell pepper

Bring apples and water to boil in heavy large saucepan. Reduce heat, cover and simmer until apples are falling apart, stirring occasionally, about 30 minutes. Cool 30 minutes.

Press apple mixture through fine strainer into heavy large saucepan. Puree green peppers and chilies with 2 cups sugar in processor. Add to apples. Mix in remaining 3 cups sugar and vinegar. Boil over medium heat 10 minutes to blend flavors. Add pectin and boil exactly 2 minutes. Stir in red pepper. Pour into sterilized jars and seal. Shake jars occasionally as jelly cools to distribute peppers evenly. Store in cool dry place.

Red Pepper Jelly

Makes 7 half-pints

4 large red bell peppers (about), seeded

5½ cups sugar
¾ cup distilled white or wine vinegar

⅓ cup fresh lemon juice
1 bottle liquid pectin
Paraffin (for sealing)

Finely chop peppers in processor or run through grinder. Strain, pressing lightly. Measure 2 full cups and ¼ cup pepper juice. Discard remaining juice.

Combine ground peppers, pepper juice, sugar and vinegar in 3- or 4-quart saucepan. Bring to boil, stirring frequently. Remove from heat and let stand 15 minutes. Reheat to boil, stirring frequently. Add lemon juice and return to boil for 1 minute, stirring. Add pectin and let boil 3 minutes, skimming off foam as it accumulates. Pour into jars. Seal with paraffin.

This recipe cannot be doubled.

Herbed Pear Jam

Makes about 7 cups

6 pounds slightly underripe bartlett pears, peeled and cored
1½ cups Zinfandel

1 8-ounce orange
1 6-ounce lemon

7 cups sugar
2 large bay leaves

3 tablespoons fresh lemon juice

Cut half of pears into ½-inch pieces. Finely chop remainder in processor. Combine all pears with wine in heavy large saucepan and set aside.

Using vegetable peeler, remove half of peel from orange and lemon (colored part only). Thinly slice peel. Remove remaining peel and all white pith from orange and lemon. Chop pulp finely, discarding seeds and tough membrane. Stir sliced peel and chopped pulp into pears. Cover and simmer over medium heat 10 minutes to blend flavors.

Reduce heat to low, add sugar and bay leaves to pears and cook until sugar dissolves, swirling pan occasionally. Increase heat and bring to rolling but not foaming boil. Cook about 40 minutes, stirring frequently toward end of cooking time. (To test for doneness, remove pan from heat. Fill chilled spoon with jam, then slowly pour jam back into pan; last 2 drops should merge and sheet off spoon. One tablespoon of jam ladled onto chilled plate and frozen 2 minutes should wrinkle when pushed with finger.)

Stir in lemon juice; discard bay leaves. Spoon jam into hot jar to 1/4 inch from top. Immediately wipe rim using towel dipped in hot water. Place lid on jar; seal tightly. Repeat with remaining jars. Arrange jars in large pot. Cover with boiling water by at least 1 inch. Cover pot and boil 15 minutes.

Remove jars from water bath. Cool to room temperature. Press center of each lid. If lid stays down, jar is sealed. Store in cool dry place for up to 1 year. Refrigerate after opening. (If lid pops up, store jam in refrigerator.)

Marvelous Microwave Marmalade

Makes about 2/3 cup

1 navel orange (unpeeled),
  quartered
Sugar

Shred orange in processor. Measure shredded orange and transfer to 1-quart glass bowl. Measure enough sugar to equal amount of orange. Add to bowl. Cook on medium until slightly thickened, stirring occasionally, about 6 minutes; do not overcook. Cover marmalade and refrigerate until ready to use.

Red Onion and Rosemary Marmalade with Cassis

This versatile mixture goes well with roast beef, pork, ham, turkey, duck or grilled sausages. For maximum flavor, make at least one week ahead.

Makes about 8 cups

1 cup sugar
3/4 cup red wine vinegar
2 cups dry white wine
1/3 cup olive oil
1 teaspoon salt
6 pounds red onions, halved and
  thinly sliced

3/4 cup dried currants
2 tablespoons tomato paste
2 tablespoons fresh rosemary leaves
2 teaspoons dried thyme leaves
1/3 cup crème de cassis

Cook sugar in heavy large nonaluminum saucepan over low heat until golden brown, about 20 minutes. Remove from heat and let stand 2 minutes. Add vinegar (be careful; mixture may splatter). Swirl pan over medium-high heat until sugar dissolves, about 5 minutes. Add wine, olive oil and salt and simmer 3 minutes. Add onions, pushing down into liquid. Reduce heat, cover pan partially and simmer until onions soften, 45 minutes.

Stir currants, tomato paste, rosemary and thyme into onion mixture and cook until liquid is syrupy, about 30 minutes. Stir in crème de cassis and cook 5 minutes. Ladle marmalade into hot jars. Cool, then seal jars. Refrigerate. Let stand at room temperature 20 minutes before serving.

Amber Clove Citrus Marmalade

Makes about 5¹/₂ cups

1 pound white grapefruit	1 teaspoon whole cloves
3 medium oranges (1¹/₂ pounds total)	4¹/₂ cups sugar
³/₄ pound lemons	
6 quarts cold water	

Discard tops and bottoms of grapefruits, 2 oranges and lemons. Score fruits vertically at 1-inch intervals and peel. Remove all but ¹/₁₆ inch white pith from peel. Cut peel crosswise into ¹/₁₆-inch-wide strips. Bring 2 quarts water and peel to boil in medium saucepan. Cook 5 minutes; drain. Repeat process with another 2 quarts water.

Remove peel and white pith from remaining orange and all white pith from peeled fruits. Chop pulp finely, removing seeds and tough membrane; do not discard. Tie seeds, membrane and cloves in cheesecloth. Combine blanched peel, cheesecloth bag and remaining 2 quarts water in large saucepan and bring to boil. Boil 5 minutes. Cover and let stand at room temperature overnight.

Uncover saucepan, bring mixture to medium boil and cook until mixture is reduced to 6 cups, about 30 minutes. Let cool for 10 minutes.

Remove cheesecloth bag, pressing to extract juice into mixture. Add sugar and stir until dissolved. Ladle half of mixture into heavy medium saucepan. Bring to rolling but not foaming boil and cook about 20 minutes, stirring frequently toward end. (To test for doneness, remove pan from heat. Fill chilled spoon with marmalade, then slowly pour back into pan; last 2 drops should merge and sheet off spoon. One tablespoon ladled onto chilled plate and frozen 2 minutes should wrinkle when pushed with finger.)

Spoon marmalade into hot jar to ¹/₄ inch from top. Immediately wipe rim using towel dipped in hot water. Place lid on jar; seal tightly. Repeat with remaining jars. Repeat entire process with remaining half of marmalade. Arrange jars in large pot. Cover with boiling water by at least 1 inch. Cover pot and boil 15 minutes.

Remove jars from water bath. Cool to room temperature. Press center of each lid. If lid stays down, jar is sealed. Store in cool dry place for up to 1 year. Refrigerate after opening. (If lid pops up, store marmalade in refrigerator.)

For variation, omit cloves. Cool finished marmalade 2 minutes, then stir in 3 tablespoons Cognac. Spoon marmalade into hot jars and process as above.

Five-Fruit Marmalade

For best flavor, use thin-skinned fruit.

Makes about 8 pints

2 medium lemons, quartered and seeded (do not peel)	1 large pineapple, peeled, cored and cut into 8 wedges
2 medium limes, quartered and seeded (do not peel)	2 quarts water
1 large orange, quartered and seeded (do not peel)	7 cups sugar
1 large grapefruit, quartered and seeded (do not peel)	

Thinly slice cut-up lemons, limes, oranges, grapefruit and pineapple. Remove any remaining seeds. Transfer fruit to nonmetallic bowl. Pour water over fruit and let stand overnight.

Transfer undrained fruit to heavy, wide, large Dutch oven. Bring to boil over medium-high heat. Let boil 15 minutes, then set aside 24 hours.

Stir sugar into fruit mixture. Bring to boil over medium-high heat. Reduce heat and simmer until thickened, stirring occasionally, about 1 hour. Meanwhile, immerse eight 1-pint jars in boiling water. Boil for 15 minutes; keep immersed until ready to use. Ladle marmalade into 1 hot jar to $1/2$-inch from top. Run plastic knife or spatula between marmalade and jar to release any air bubbles. Clean rim and threads of jar with damp cloth. Seal with new, scalded, very hot lid. Repeat with remaining jars. Let jars cool on rack. Test for seal. Store in cool dry place for up to 1 year. Refrigerate after opening.

Gingered Cranberry-Grapefruit Marmalade

Makes about 6 cups

2 pounds white grapefruit
$5^1/2$ quarts cold water

4 cups sugar

1 12-ounce bag cranberries
$1/2$ cup minced crystallized ginger

Discard tops and bottoms of grapefruits. Score grapefruits vertically at 1-inch intervals and peel. Remove all but $1/16$ inch white pith from peel. Cut peel crosswise into $1/16$-inch-wide strips. Bring 2 quarts water and peel to boil in medium saucepan. Cook 5 minutes, then drain. Repeat blanching process with another 2 quarts water.

Remove all white pith from grapefruits. Chop pulp, removing seeds and tough membrane; do not discard. Tie seeds and membrane in cheesecloth. Combine blanched peel, pulp, cheesecloth bag and remaining $1^1/2$ quarts water in heavy large saucepan and bring to boil. Let boil 5 minutes. Cover and let stand at room temperature overnight to blend flavors.

Uncover saucepan, bring mixture to medium boil and cook until pulp and peel are very tender, about 20 minutes. Cool 10 minutes. Remove cheesecloth bag, pressing to extract juice into mixture. Add sugar and stir until dissolved. Bring mixture to rolling but not foaming boil and cook about 20 minutes, stirring frequently toward end of cooking time. (To test for doneness, remove pan from heat. Fill chilled spoon with marmalade, then slowly pour back into pan; last 2 drops should merge and sheet off spoon. One tablespoon on chilled plate, frozen 2 minutes, should wrinkle when pushed with finger.)

Mix in cranberries and boil until just beginning to pop, about 2 minutes. Stir in ginger. Spoon marmalade into hot jar to $1/4$ inch from top. Immediately wipe rim using towel dipped in hot water. Place lid on jar; seal tightly. Repeat with remaining jars. Arrange jars in large pot. Cover with boiling water by at least 1 inch. Cover pot and boil rapidly for 15 minutes.

Remove jars from water bath. Cool to room temperature. Press center of each lid. If lid stays down, jar is sealed. Store in cool dry place for up to 1 year. Refrigerate after opening. (If lid pops up, store marmalade in refrigerator.)

Chunky Apricot Preserves

This easy preserve makes delightful gifts.

Makes about 3½ cups

1 6-ounce package dried apricots
1 cup water
4 cups sugar
1 8¼-ounce can crushed pineapple packed in its own juice, undrained

1 10-ounce package frozen yellow squash, thawed and drained (optional)

Combine apricots and water in medium saucepan and let stand about 1 hour to plump. Place over medium heat and cook until apricots are tender, about 10 minutes. Mash into coarse chunks. Add sugar, pineapple and squash, blending well. Continue cooking over low heat until mixture is thickened, stirring occasionally, about 15 minutes. Pour into sterilized jars and seal. Let cool. Store preserves in refrigerator.

Loquat-Apple Preserves

Using slightly underripe loquats will lend an appealing tartness to the preserves. The riper the loquats, the sweeter the results will be.

Makes 5 cups

2 pounds sugar
1 pound loquats, pitted, pithed and finely chopped

1 pound Granny Smith apples, cored and finely chopped
½ cup water

Combine all ingredients in heavy large saucepan and bring to boil over low heat. Simmer until preserves thicken and are amber color, stirring often, about 2 hours. Let cool. Ladle into sterilized jars and seal.

Cranberry Cassis Preserves

Makes about 4 cups

3 cups sugar
¾ cup water
4½ cups cranberries
2 medium apples, peeled, cored and coarsely diced

1 tablespoon grated lemon peel
¼ to ⅓ cup crème de cassis

Heat sugar and water in heavy large saucepan over low heat, swirling pan occasionally, until sugar dissolves. Add cranberries, apples and lemon peel. Bring to boil. Reduce heat to medium and cook until consistency of thick jam, stirring frequently, about 20 minutes. Stir in cassis to taste. Cool completely before serving. (*Can be stored in refrigerator 1 month.*)

Viennese Beet Preserves

Makes 3 pints

2 pounds beets, leaves trimmed to 2 inches
3 cups sugar (1½ pounds)

1 tablespoon ground ginger
3 small lemons, very finely chopped
1 cup finely chopped almonds

Cook whole beets in boiling water until tender, about 30 minutes. Let cool; peel and dice. Combine diced beets, sugar and ginger in medium saucepan and cook over medium-low heat 30 minutes. Add chopped lemon and continue cooking until slightly thickened, stirring occasionally to prevent sticking, about 30 minutes. Stir in almonds. Transfer to jars with tight-fitting lids and seal. Store in cool, dark place.

A selection of savory mustards perfect for gift giving

Alan Krosnick

Clockwise from left: Maple Syrup
Shortbreads; Brandied Cherries; Apple
Pepper Jelly; Japanese Kumquat Sauce;
Old-Fashioned Gingerbread House;
Serpentona; Certosino (fruitcake
from Bologna)

Marvelous Microwave Marmalade

*Collect pleasingly shaped bottles and
decanters to fill with flavored vinegars and
oils for an impressive gift presentation.*

Clockwise from top right: Macadamia Nut Fudge; Mint Truffles; Chocolate-coated Cherry Surprises; Chocolate Peanut Clusters; Date and Peanut Butter Balls

Red Pepper Relish and Italian Pickled
Vegetables (Giardiniera)

🍎 *Perfect Preserves*

Tips to Getting Started

Carefully sort your produce for size and ripeness so it will cook evenly. Wash well in small batches and drain thoroughly, then trim any bruised or soft spots and peel if necessary. Cut into uniform pieces. Have food and equipment ready: a good supply of commercial canning jars with matching two-piece dome lids, a water-bath canner with a rack that keeps jars from coming in contact with the bottom of the pan and plenty of coarse salt and sugar.

Necessary equipment is minimal. Recommended are one or two wide, heavy kettles with thick bottoms (do not use cast-iron, which will react with brine) that are deep enough for the jars to be immersed completely and surrounded by hot water, several widemouth funnels, and ladles of assorted sizes. Canning jars without chips and rings may be reused from one year to the next, but new dome lids are a must. Pincer tongs and jar-lifting tongs are essential. A scale is a helpful option, as is a jelly or canning thermometer.

After filling the jars and processing them, don't be alarmed if you hear pops and pings as they cool; that lets you know they are sealing nicely. Any jars that do not seal should be refrigerated and the contents used within a reasonable period of time; vegetables pickled in brine keep well in the refrigerator for months. Well-sealed home-processed products keep best—and indefinitely—in a cool dark basement or garage. However, a normal kitchen cupboard works well for a year, although there may be some color fading, which is not harmful. If there is any questionable appearance or odor when a jar is opened, discard the contents immediately without tasting.

Do not change the cooking time or alter the proportions of sugar, vinegar or salt in these recipes, as those ingredients are necessary for preservation and flavor. But feel free to experiment with the amounts of herbs, spices, peppers and garlic to suit your taste.

Step by Step to Perfect Preserving

- Select jars and clean thoroughly in hot soapy water; keep hot.
- Place dome lids and sealing rings in pan of simmering water.
- Ladle hot prepared mixture into jars, arranging attractively and filling to within one-half inch of top. Pack jars as full as possible.
- Check for air pockets by running thin plastic knife or spatula, or chopstick, between mixture and jar.
- Clean rims and threads of jars with damp cloth to ensure a seal. Place dome lids on jars and screw on rings.
- Transfer jars to canner or heavy Dutch oven with enough very hot water to cover the lids by at least one inch. Simmer gently at 180°F to 190°F for amount of time specified in the recipe; *do not boil.*
- Transfer jars to towels or wire rack to cool (contact with a cold surface could cause hot jars to crack), spacing well apart so air can circulate. Cool several hours or overnight.
- Test for seal by pressing center of each lid. If the dome is down or stays down when pressed, there is a good seal. (Occasionally a jar may not seal for 24 hours, so be patient.)

Prune-Port Butter

Makes about 6 cups

1 medium orange, thinly sliced
1 2¹/₂-inch cinnamon stick, halved
¹/₂ teaspoon whole cloves
¹/₂ teaspoon whole allspice
2 pounds pitted prunes, halved

3 cups fresh orange juice
3 cups ruby Port

1 cup sugar
Pinch of salt

Tie orange, cinnamon, cloves and allspice in cheesecloth. Place in heavy medium saucepan. Add prunes, orange juice and Port and bring to boil. Reduce heat, cover and simmer until prunes are softened, about 30 minutes. Let mixture stand at room temperature overnight to blend flavors.

Discard cheesecloth bag. Puree prune mixture in processor or blender in batches until smooth. Return to saucepan. Blend in sugar and salt. Stir over low heat until sugar dissolves. Increase heat to medium and boil until mixture mounds slightly on spoon, stirring frequently, about 10 minutes.

Spoon butter into hot jar to ¹/₄ inch from top. Immediately wipe rim using towel dipped in hot water. Place lid on jar; seal tightly. Repeat with remaining jars. Arrange jars in large pot. Cover with boiling water by at least 1 inch. Cover pot and boil 15 minutes.

Remove jars from water bath. Cool to room temperature. Press center of each lid. If lid stays down, jar is sealed. Store in cool dry place for up to 1 year. Refrigerate after opening. (If lid pops up, store butter in refrigerator.)

Pear Vanilla Butter

Mix with softly whipped cream for an easy and delicious dessert.

Makes about 4 cups

4 pounds bartlett pears, cored and
 cut into 1-inch chunks
¹/₂ cup dry white wine
3 tablespoons fresh lemon juice

1¹/₂ cups sugar
1 4-inch vanilla bean, split

1 2¹/₂-inch cinnamon stick
1 lemon slice
¹/₈ teaspoon salt

2 tablespoons Cognac

Combine pears with wine and 2 tablespoons lemon juice in heavy medium saucepan. Cover and simmer until pears are soft, pushing into liquid occasionally, about 20 minutes. Force mixture through medium disc of food mill to remove peel. Transfer to processor and puree until smooth.

Cook pear puree, sugar, vanilla bean, cinnamon, lemon slice and salt in heavy medium saucepan over low heat until sugar dissolves, swirling pan occasionally. Increase heat to medium and boil gently until mixture thickens and mounds slightly on spoon, stirring frequently, about 40 minutes.

Discard vanilla bean, cinnamon and lemon slice. Stir in remaining 1 tablespoon lemon juice and Cognac. Spoon butter into hot jar to ¹/₄ inch from top. Immediately wipe rim using towel dipped in hot water. Place lid on jar; seal tightly. Repeat with remaining jars. Arrange jars in large pot. Cover with boiling water by at least 1 inch. Cover pot and boil rapidly 15 minutes.

Remove jars from water bath. Cool to room temperature. Press center of each lid. If lid stays down, jar is sealed. Store in cool dry place for up to 1 year. Refrigerate after opening. (If lid pops up, store butter in refrigerator.)

Apple-Cardamom Butter

Makes about 5 1/2 cups

3 pounds unpeeled Rome Beauty
  apples, cut into 1-inch chunks
1 pound unpeeled Granny Smith
  apples, cut into 1-inch chunks
1 1/2 cups apple juice

2 cups firmly packed light brown
  sugar

1 5-inch vanilla bean, split
1 tablespoon dark molasses
1 teaspoon grated orange peel
1/4 teaspoon crushed cardamom seed

Combine apples and apple juice in heavy large saucepan and bring to boil. Reduce heat, cover and simmer until apples are tender, pushing into liquid occasionally, about 20 minutes.

Force mixture through medium disc of food mill into heavy large saucepan. Mix in remaining ingredients. Stir over low heat until sugar dissolves. Increase heat and simmer 20 minutes to blend flavors, stirring frequently. Cover and let stand at room temperature overnight to blend flavors.

Bring to boil over medium heat and cook until mixture mounds slightly on spoon, stirring often, about 15 minutes.

Discard vanilla bean. Spoon butter into hot jar to 1/4 inch from top. Immediately wipe rim using towel dipped in hot water. Place lid on jar; seal tightly. Repeat with remaining jars. Arrange jars in large pot. Cover with boiling water by at least 1 inch. Cover pot and boil rapidly 15 minutes.

Remove jars from water bath. Cool to room temperature. Press center of each lid. If lid stays down, jar is sealed. Store in cool dry place for up to 1 year. Refrigerate after opening. (If lid pops up, store butter in refrigerator.)

Bachelor's Confiture

This combination of seasonal fruit soaked in vodka and sugar should mellow for at least two months for maximum flavor. As you use the confiture, add more fruit, vodka and sugar to keep a steady supply. The charming name derives from the fact that in the Périgord, this vodka-spiked mixture is felt to be suitable only for male dinner guests; it is frequently served during the autumn hunting season.

Makes about 2 pounds

2 pounds peaches, plums, apricots,
  prunes, pears, apples, figs,
  strawberries, raspberries, cherries,
  grapes and currants or any
  combination

1 750-ml bottle (or more) vodka
2 pounds sugar
1 large lemon, cut into 1/8-inch
  slices

Peel and pit peaches; cut into eighths. Pit plums, apricots and prunes; cut into sixths. Halve and core pears and apples; cut into eighths. Halve figs. Leave remaining fruit whole.

Pour vodka into large glass jar with lid. Add sugar and stir to dissolve. Add fruit. Pour in more vodka if necessary to cover fruit completely. Let stand in cool dry place for at least 2 months, stirring occasionally and adding more vodka, fruit, sugar and lemon as desired to replenish supply.

Spiked Fruit Compote

Makes about 4 cups

3¹/₂ cups water
3¹/₂ tablespoons sugar
4 whole cloves
1 1-inch cinnamon stick
2 ounces dried pear halves, halved (¹/₂ cup)
2 ounces dried peach halves, halved (¹/₂ cup)
1¹/₂ ounces dried apple slices, halved (¹/₂ cup)

3 ounces dried pitted prunes (¹/₂ cup)
2 ounces dried apricots (¹/₂ cup)
¹/₄ cup Armagnac, Cognac or orange liqueur

Bring 2¹/₂ cups water, 2 tablespoons sugar, cloves and cinnamon to boil in heavy medium saucepan. Add pears, peaches and apples. Reduce heat, cover and simmer until softened, about 15 minutes. Add remaining water, 1 tablespoon sugar, prunes and apricots. Cover and simmer until fruit is tender, about 15 minutes. Pour into bowl. Stir in remaining ¹/₂ tablespoon sugar and Armagnac. Cool completely. Cover and refrigerate at least 2 days. Remove cloves and cinnamon. Rewarm fruit slightly and serve.

Apricots in Rum with Ginger and Sultanas

For gift giving, tuck a jar of this rum-laced fruit mixture into a pretty basket lined with a linen towel; accompany with liqueur glasses or dessert spoons. Superb over vanilla ice cream or pound cake slices, or use as a filling for omelets and crepes. A small glass of the liquid makes a delightfully different after-dinner liqueur.

Makes about 7 cups

2 pounds plump dried apricots
6 cups warm brewed orange pekoe tea
1¹/₂ cups sultanas (golden raisins)
1¹/₂ cups sugar
³/₄ cup water

4 2-inch cinnamon sticks
8 ¹/₄-inch-thick fresh ginger slices
18 whole allspice

2 to 4 cups imported golden rum

Combine apricots and 4 cups warm tea in deep bowl. Let stand until plump but not soft, 2 to 5 hours, depending on moistness of apricots. Plump raisins in remaining 2 cups tea 30 minutes. Drain apricots and raisins separately. Transfer to paper towels.

Cook sugar and water in heavy medium saucepan over low heat, swirling pan occasionally, until sugar dissolves. Increase heat and boil 3 minutes. Stir in cinnamon, ginger and allspice. Let cool to room temperature.

Layer apricots and raisins in jars. Remove cinnamon, ginger and allspice from syrup; divide spices among hot jars, arranging so they show on sides. Divide syrup among jars. Fill jars with rum, leaving ¹/₄-inch space at top. Seal jars tightly. Turn jars several times to mix. Refrigerate 2 weeks before using. (*Can be stored in refrigerator 4 months. Top with additional rum when liquid falls below surface of apricots and sultanas.*)

Brandied Cherries

Delicious spooned over fresh fruit, ice cream, crepes or waffles. Apricots are also nice prepared this way.

Makes about 2²/₃ cups

1 pound fresh or frozen cherries, pitted

¹/₃ cup sugar
1¹/₂ cups (about) brandy

Place cherries in sterilized jar. Add sugar and enough brandy to cover. Cover tightly and shake to mix ingredients. Refrigerate 2 months before serving to mellow flavors, shaking well once a day for 4 days.

Peaches in Brandy

Makes 2 quarts

3 pounds firm, just-ripe peaches (about 12 medium peaches)
Boiling water

1¹/₂ cups sugar
1 cup water

2 to 3 cups brandy

Prepare jars. Dip peaches into boiling water 30 to 60 seconds to loosen skin. Immediately plunge into cold water. Peel, halve and remove pits.

Combine sugar and water in small saucepan and cook over low heat, stirring occasionally, until sugar is dissolved. Increase heat and bring to boil. Let boil 5 minutes. Remove from heat.

Firmly pack peaches pitted side down into hot sterilized jars. Add enough syrup so it is between ¹/₃ to ¹/₂ full. Add brandy to within ¹/₂ inch of top and seal. Process 25 minutes in boiling water bath. Remove from water and let cool. Test for seal. Let stand in cool dark place at least 3 months before serving. Refrigerate after opening.

Eau de Vie de Poire

Makes 3 quarts

2 cups sugar
1¹/₃ cups water

5 to 6 pounds ripe pears (about 11 medium pears), peeled, cored and quartered

Brandy

Prepare jars. Combine sugar and water in small saucepan and cook over low heat, stirring occasionally, until sugar is dissolved. Increase heat and bring to boil; boil 5 minutes. Remove from heat.

Firmly pack pears cored side down into hot sterilized jars. Add enough syrup to come ¹/₃ up sides of jars. Add enough brandy to cover fruit completely. Seal jars. Process 25 minutes in boiling water bath. Remove from water and let cool. Test for seal. Let stand in cool dark place at least 3 months before serving. Refrigerate after opening.

Pineapple in Brandy

Makes 4 quarts

2 to 3 large ripe pineapples (6 pounds after peeling and coring)

Sugar
Brandy

Peel pineapples. Depending on jars being used, slice into rings and core (to fit wide-mouthed jars), or cut into wedges, core and slice. Half-fill hot sterilized jars. Add enough sugar to come halfway up sides of jars; add remaining pineapple, packing well. Add brandy to within ½ inch of top and seal. Process 25 minutes in boiling water bath. Remove from water and let stand until cooled. Test for seal. Let pineapple stand in cool dark place at least 3 months before serving. Refrigerate after opening.

Spiced Damson Plums

Makes about 5 quarts

6 pounds damson plums
5 to 6 cinnamon sticks, broken into 1-inch pieces
20 whole cloves
15 currant leaves or rose geranium leaves

6 pints distilled white vinegar
3 pounds sugar

Rinse plums and pat dry. Prick outside surfaces well with wooden pick to prevent shrinkage. Pack plums into sterilized jars, layering with cinnamon sticks, cloves and currant leaves.

Heat vinegar and sugar in heavy-bottomed very large saucepan over medium-low heat until sugar dissolves, swirling pan occasionally. Increase heat to medium-high and simmer 15 minutes. Pour simmering syrup over plums. Seal jars tightly with sterilized new lids. Let spiced plums stand in cool dark place 8 to 12 weeks before using.

For variation, substitute cherries for plums.

Brandied Prunes

Makes about 3 pints

1½ cups sugar
1 cup water

2 pounds dried extra large prunes (with pits)

Peel of 1 large orange
Cinnamon sticks
1½ to 2 cups brandy

Combine sugar and water in small saucepan and cook over low heat, stirring occasionally, until sugar is dissolved. Increase heat, bring to boil and let boil 5 minutes. Keep hot.

Fill hot sterilized widemouthed jars ²/₃ full with prunes. Push several strips of orange peel into fruit and add a cinnamon stick to each jar. Pour enough syrup into each jar so it is between ½ to ²/₃ full. Add brandy to within ½ inch of top and seal. Process 25 minutes in boiling water bath. Remove from water and let cool. Test for seal. Let stand in cool dark place at least 3 months before serving. Refrigerate after opening.

6 ❦ Breads, Cakes and Cookies

Everyone likes to bake—the process of mixing the dough, working it with your hands and finally taking out of the oven a wholesome loaf of bread or a rich pastry swirled with spices and filled with rich fruits and nuts is immensely satisfying. And baked goods are always a favorite gift. Whether you're making a simple country loaf or a fancy fruitbread or cookies, these home-baked goodies are sure to please.

The winter holidays are perhaps the most popular time for gifts of bread and cookies, from German Dresden Stollen (page 77) and Nürnberger Lebkuchen Bars with Lemon Glaze (page 96), to English Plum Pudding (page 85) and all-American Jumbo Ginger Breadmen (page 81). But these baked treats are so good you will want to make and give them at other times of the year as well. Use a batch of Maytag Blue Cheese Shortbread (page 66) as a hostess gift, or try Sesame Streusel Cake (page 84) instead of toast at breakfast.

Plain or fancy, breads and cakes look best when given a special gift-wrapping. Present bread in a colorful gingham cloth or in simple brown paper tied with bright ribbons. Collect fancy molds, cake tins and decorative boxes for cookies and cakes. Whatever you use as packaging, make it fun and colorful—and be sure to protect baked goods by first wrapping them tightly in plastic.

Crackers and Breads

LBJ Ranch Cheese Wafers

Makes about 6 dozen

2 cups all purpose flour
1 teaspoon cayenne pepper
$1/2$ teaspoon salt
1 cup (2 sticks) butter, room temperature

8 ounces sharp cheddar cheese, grated
2 cups toasted rice cereal or finely chopped pecans

Preheat oven to 350°F. Combine flour, cayenne and salt in large bowl. Cut in butter until mixture resembles coarse meal. Mix in cheese. Fold in cereal or nuts. Form dough into 1-inch rounds. Place on ungreased baking sheets and flatten to $13/4$-inch rounds, using back of fork. Bake until light brown, 15 minutes. Cool on rack. Store in airtight container.

Hickory-Smoked Cheddar Crackers

Makes about 32

$3/4$ cup sifted all purpose flour
$1/2$ cup sifted whole wheat flour
$1/4$ cup sifted rice flour
1 teaspoon baking powder
$1/2$ teaspoon salt
$1/4$ teaspoon cayenne pepper

$1/4$ cup solidified rendered bacon drippings
6 ounces hickory-smoked cheddar cheese, grated (1 cup)
4 tablespoons (about) ice water

Sift flours, baking powder, salt and pepper into large bowl. Cut in drippings until mixture resembles coarse meal. Mix in cheese. Using fork, stir in enough water 1 tablespoon at a time so dough just comes together. Gather dough into ball. Wrap in plastic and refrigerate 10 minutes.

Preheat oven to 350°F. Butter baking sheet. Roll dough out on lightly floured surface to thickness of $1/8$ inch. Using fork, pierce entire surface. Cut out $21/2$-inch rounds or squares. Using spatula, transfer to prepared sheet. Gather scraps and refrigerate 10 minutes. Reroll and cut additional rounds or squares. Bake until crisp and golden, about 15 minutes. Transfer to rack and cool completely. (*Can be prepared 3 days ahead and stored in airtight container.*)

Indian Crackers (Matthi)

Makes about 24

$11/2$ cups unbleached all purpose flour
1 teaspoon coarse kosher salt
$1/2$ teaspoon black onion seed* or $3/4$ teaspoon cumin seed
$1/4$ teaspoon cayenne pepper
6 tablespoons solid vegetable shortening
$1/3$ cup water

Peanut oil or corn oil for deep frying

Combine flour, salt, onion seed or cumin seed and cayenne in medium bowl. Cut in shortening until mixture resembles coarse meal. Add water and mix until firm but workable dough forms. Knead dough on lightly floured surface 1 minute; be careful not to overwork.

Divide dough into thirds. Roll 1 piece out on floured surface to ⅛-inch-thick round, dusting with flour to prevent sticking. Cut out 2-inch-round crackers, using cookie cutter or glass. Using sharp knife, cut six ¼-inch-long slashes in center of each. Repeat with remaining dough. Gather scraps, reroll and cut additional crackers.

Pour oil into deep fryer or deep skillet to depth of 1½ inches. Heat to 350°F. Add crackers to oil in batches and cook until just beginning to color, turning constantly, about 2 minutes. Transfer to paper towels using slotted spoon. Cool completely. (*Can be stored in airtight container up to 2 months.*)

*Available at Indian markets.

Rosemary-Dill Breadsticks

These flavorful breadsticks are best the same day they are baked.

Makes 14

4 cups (about) all purpose flour	2 tablespoons minced fresh
1⅓ cups warm water (105°F to 115°F)	rosemary
1 envelope dry yeast	2 tablespoons minced fresh dill
2 tablespoons olive oil	
1 egg beaten with 2 tablespoons water	Coarse salt

Mix 2 cups flour with water and yeast in large bowl until smooth. Add oil, 2 tablespoons egg mixture (reserve remainder for glaze), rosemary and dill. Mix in enough remaining flour ½ cup at a time to form soft dough. Knead on floured surface until smooth and elastic, adding more flour if sticky, about 8 minutes. Grease large bowl. Add dough, turning to coat entire surface. Cover and let rest in warm, draft-free area for 30 minutes.

Preheat oven to 400°F. Grease baking sheet. Divide dough in half. Roll each piece into 18-inch-long rope. Cut each rope into 14 pieces. Roll each piece into 12-inch-long rope. Twist 2 ropes together. Arrange on prepared sheet. Repeat with remaining dough ropes. Brush with reserved egg mixture. Sprinkle with coarse salt. Bake until breadsticks are golden brown, about 20 minutes. Cool on rack before serving.

Sage Cheddar Breadsticks

Makes 56

½ cup milk	¾ cup grated sage Derby cheese
¼ cup water	1 egg white, beaten to blend
2 tablespoons corn oil	1 cup (about) sesame seed
1 envelope dry yeast	
1 tablespoon sugar	
2 cups all purpose flour	
1 teaspoon salt	

Bring milk, water and oil to boil in heavy small saucepan. Let cool to 85°F. Stir in yeast and sugar. Combine flour and salt in large bowl. Make well in center. Add yeast mixture to well. Using fork, gradually incorporate flour until soft dough forms. Turn dough out onto generously floured surface and knead for 5 minutes.

Oil large bowl. Add dough, turning to coat entire surface. Cover and let rise in warm draft-free area until doubled in volume, about 1¼ hours.

Lightly butter baking sheets. Sprinkle dough with cheese. Punch dough down. Knead lightly to incorporate cheese. Divide dough in half. Keep one half covered. Roll remainder out on lightly floured surface into 8 × 14-inch rectangle about ¼ inch thick. Cut dough lengthwise into 4 pieces. Cut dough crosswise into 2-inch pieces. Roll each piece into 4-inch stick about ½ inch in diameter. Brush each stick with egg white. Roll in sesame seeds. Arrange on prepared sheet. Repeat with remaining dough. Cover and let rise in warm draft-free area until almost doubled, about 30 minutes.

Preheat oven to 400°F. Bake sticks until browned, about 15 minutes. Cool slightly on rack before serving.

Maytag Blue Cheese Shortbread

Makes about 4½ dozen

¾ cup (1½ sticks) butter, room temperature
8 ounces Maytag blue cheese, room temperature
¼ cup sugar

2 cups sifted all purpose flour
½ cup sifted rice flour
Pinch of salt

Preheat oven to 350°F. Using electric mixer, cream butter and cheese. Gradually add sugar and beat until light and creamy. Slowly add flours and salt and beat just to combine; do not overbeat. Spread mixture evenly onto 9 × 12-inch baking sheet. Using fork, pierce entire surface. Using back of knife, mark off finger-size rectangles on dough. Bake until light golden, about 25 minutes; do not brown. Immediately cut through dough to mark off rectangles; do not separate. Cool completely in pan. Separate into rectangles before serving. (*Can be prepared 3 days ahead and stored in airtight container in cool dry place.*)

Cheese-Almond Diamonds

Makes about 4 dozen

8 ounces finely grated cheddar cheese
1 cup (2 sticks) butter, room temperature
1 tablespoon caraway seed
½ teaspoon salt
½ teaspoon freshly ground pepper

1¾ cups plus 3 tablespoons all purpose flour
2 tablespoons cornstarch
48 (about) blanched almonds

Preheat oven to 325°F. Lightly grease baking sheets. Mix cheese, butter, caraway seed, salt and pepper in large bowl until light and fluffy. Sift together flour and cornstarch and add to cheese mixture. Shape into 1-inch balls. Transfer to prepared baking sheets. Flatten slightly and press almond into center of each. Pinch corners to form diamond shapes. Bake until lightly browned, 10 to 15 minutes. Cool completely. Store in airtight container.

Della Robbia Loaf

An impressive glazed country bread decorated like a holiday wreath. Prepare the doughs one after the other so rising times will coincide.

Makes 1 loaf

Dough No. 1
- 2 envelopes dry yeast
- 2 tablespoons sugar
- 1/2 cup warm water (105°F to 115°F)
- 1/2 cup (1 stick) unsalted butter, room temperature
- 1/2 cup warm milk
- 3 eggs, room temperature
- 2 teaspoons salt
- 4 to 4 1/2 cups all purpose flour

Dough No. 2
- 1 envelope dry yeast
- 1 tablespoon sugar
- 1/4 cup warm water (105°F to 115°F)
- 1/4 cup (1/2 stick) unsalted butter, room temperature
- 2 eggs, room temperature
- 1/4 cup warm milk
- 1 teaspoon salt
- 2 to 2 1/4 cups all purpose flour

- 1 egg beaten with 1 tablespoon water (glaze)
- 2 tablespoons minced fresh rosemary or 2 teaspoons dried, crumbled

For dough no. 1: Sprinkle yeast and sugar over warm water in large bowl and stir until yeast is dissolved. Let stand until foamy, about 10 minutes. Blend in butter, milk, eggs and salt. Stir in 2 cups flour. Stir in another 2 cups flour. Turn dough out onto floured surface. Knead in enough of remaining flour to form soft but not sticky dough. Continue kneading 1 minute. Shape into round. Cover and let stand 10 minutes. Knead dough until smooth and elastic, about 10 minutes. Butter large bowl. Add dough, turning to coat entire surface. Cover and let rise in warm draft-free area until doubled in volume, about 2 hours.

For dough no. 2: Sprinkle yeast and sugar over warm water in large bowl and let stand until dissolved; stir to blend. Let stand until foamy, about 10 minutes. Blend in butter, eggs, milk and salt. Stir in 1 cup flour. Stir in another 1 cup flour. Turn dough out onto floured surface. Knead in enough of remaining flour to form soft but not sticky dough. Continue kneading 1 minute. Shape into round. Cover and let stand 10 minutes. Knead dough until smooth and elastic, about 10 minutes. Butter large bowl. Add dough, turning to coat entire surface. Cover and let rise in warm draft-free area until doubled in volume, about 2 hours.

To assemble: Generously butter 14 × 2-inch round baking pan.* Punch dough no. 1 down. Gently roll into 14-inch round. Fit into prepared pan. Punch dough no. 2 down. Cut into 9 pieces. Using hands, lightly roll 8 pieces into 6-inch leaf-shaped lengths with pointed ends. Arrange lengths equidistant atop dough in pan. Roll remaining piece into 6-inch cylinder. Arrange in spiral in pan. Cover and let rise in warm draft-free area until doubled, about 1 hour.

Preheat oven to 375°F. Brush loaf with glaze. Sprinkle with rosemary. Bake until lightly browned, about 35 minutes. Cool slightly in pan. Turn out onto rack and cool completely.

*If unavailable, wrap 14-inch pizza pan with 2-inch heavy foil collar.

Minnie's Challah

An heirloom recipe.

Makes 2 loaves

3 ounces unsalted margarine, cut into pieces
1 cup water
5½ cups all purpose flour
¼ cup sugar
2 envelopes dry yeast

2 teaspoons salt
4 eggs
1 egg, separated

Boiling water

½ teaspoon water

Grease large ovenproof glass bowl and set aside. Melt margarine with 1 cup water in small saucepan over low heat. Let cool to lukewarm. Place 2 cups flour in large bowl of electric mixer and make well in center. Combine sugar, yeast and salt in well. Add melted margarine mixture. Using dough hook, blend at low speed until thoroughly combined, 2 to 3 minutes. Add 4 eggs and egg yolk 1 at a time, blending well at medium-low speed after each addition. Continue mixing until dough resembles thick batter, about 7 minutes. Blend in 3 cups flour ¼ cup at a time, mixing at low speed until dough is heavy and sticky and pulls away from sides of bowl, about 7 minutes. Sprinkle remaining ½ cup flour on work surface. Turn dough out onto floured surface and knead until smooth and elastic, about 5 minutes. (Dough will be sticky.) Transfer dough to prepared ovenproof glass bowl, turning to coat entire surface.

Pour boiling water into medium ovenproof glass bowl. Set large bowl with dough atop medium bowl; do not allow bottom of large bowl to touch boiling water. Cover dough with cloth and let rise in warm draft-free area until doubled in volume, 40 to 50 minutes.

Grease 2 baking sheets, or two 9 × 5-inch loaf pans, or 1 of each. Divide dough in half. Separate each half into thirds. Roll into ropes 12 to 13 inches long. Make 2 braids with ropes, tucking ends under. Transfer loaves to prepared pans. Pour boiling water into 2 medium ovenproof glass bowls. Arrange pans with loaves over water. Cover and let rise in warm draft-free area until doubled, about 30 minutes.

Preheat oven to 400°F. Remove loaves from over water. Bake until golden, about 15 minutes. Combine egg white and ½ teaspoon water and brush over loaves. Continue baking until browned, 8 to 10 minutes. Turn loaves out onto racks and cool slightly. Serve warm; or cool completely, wrap with plastic and store at room temperature.

Anadama Rolls with Orange Butter

As the folklore goes, "Anna, damn her," was apparently quite a baker. This variation on an early American bread produces delicious light rolls. Present the Orange Butter in a decorative crock.

Makes 16 rolls

2 cups milk
½ cup yellow cornmeal
⅓ cup unsulphured molasses

1 envelope dry yeast
1 cup whole wheat flour
2 teaspoons salt
2½ cups (about) unbleached all purpose flour

2 tablespoons (¼ stick) unsalted butter, room temperature

¼ cup cornmeal

1 egg, beaten to blend
Orange Butter*

Slowly whisk milk into ½ cup cornmeal in heavy small saucepan. Bring to boil over low heat, stirring constantly. Transfer to medium bowl. Stir in molasses. Cool to 105°F to 115°F.

Stir yeast into cornmeal mixture. Let stand 5 minutes. Add whole wheat flour and salt. Mix in enough all purpose flour 1/2 cup at a time to form sticky but kneadable dough. Knead on floured surface until soft, elastic and slightly sticky, adding all purpose flour if very sticky, about 10 minutes.

Grease large bowl with 2 tablespoons butter. Add dough, turning to coat entire surface. Cover bowl with towel. Let dough rise in warm draft-free area until doubled, about 2 hours.

Punch dough down. Knead on lightly floured surface until smooth. Return to bowl. Cover and let rise again until doubled in volume, about 2 hours.

Sprinkle baking sheet with 1/4 cup cornmeal. Punch dough down. Cut into 16 pieces. Form each into ball. Transfer to prepared sheet, spacing 1 1/2 inches apart. Cover rolls with towel. Let rise until almost doubled, about 30 minutes.

Position rack in center of oven and preheat to 375°F. Brush top of rolls with egg. Bake until brown and crisp, about 20 minutes. Cool on rack. (*Can be prepared 1 day ahead. Wrap tightly. Reheat in 325°F oven about 5 minutes if desired.*) Serve rolls warm or at room temperature. Pass butter separately.

*Orange Butter

Makes about 1 cup

1 cup (2 sticks) unsalted butter, softened slightly

2 tablespoons grated orange peel

Blend butter and peel in processor until smooth. Transfer to crock or small bowl. (*Can be prepared 3 days ahead. Cover tightly and refrigerate. Bring to room temperature before serving.*)

Spiced Pumpkin Loaf

Serve this bread with whipped cream cheese.

Makes 1 loaf

1 3/4 cups all purpose flour
1 teaspoon baking powder
1 teaspoon baking soda
1/2 teaspoon salt
1 cup canned pumpkin
2/3 cup sugar
1/3 cup sour cream
1/3 cup oil
1 egg

3 tablespoons orange marmalade
1 teaspoon cinnamon
1/2 teaspoon ground ginger
1/4 teaspoon freshly grated nutmeg
1/8 teaspoon ground cloves
2/3 cup chopped walnuts

Preheat oven to 350°F. Generously grease 8 1/2 × 4 1/2-inch loaf pan. Line bottom and sides with waxed paper.

Sift flour, baking powder, baking soda and salt in medium bowl and set aside. Combine pumpkin, sugar, sour cream, oil, egg, marmalade, cinnamon, ginger, nutmeg and cloves in large bowl of electric mixer and beat at medium speed until well blended. Reduce speed to low and gradually blend in flour mixture. Stir in nuts. Transfer batter to prepared pan, smoothing top. Bake until tester inserted in center comes out clean, about 65 minutes. Let cool in pan on rack 10 minutes. Remove loaf from pan and discard waxed paper. Let cool completely on rack.

Banana Yeast Bread

Makes one 9 × 5-inch loaf

Glaze
- 1 egg
- ¹/₂ teaspoon salt

Bread
- 1 envelope dry yeast
- ¹/₂ teaspoon light brown sugar
- ¹/₄ cup plus 2 tablespoons warm milk (105°F to 115°F)

- 2 cups bread flour
- 1 cup unbleached all purpose flour

- 1 large banana, pureed
- ¹/₄ cup (¹/₂ stick) unsalted butter, room temperature
- 1 egg
- 1¹/₂ teaspoons salt
- 2 tablespoons wheat germ

Additional wheat germ

For glaze: Mix egg with salt in processor 2 seconds; remove and set aside. Do not clean work bowl.

For bread: Oil large mixing bowl and set aside. Combine yeast and sugar with warm milk in small bowl and let stand until foamy, about 10 minutes.

Combine 1³/₄ cups bread flour, 1 cup all purpose flour, banana, butter, egg and salt in processor work bowl and mix about 10 seconds, stopping machine once to scrape down sides of bowl. With machine running, pour yeast mixture through feed tube and blend until dough forms ball, about 40 seconds. If dough is too wet, mix in remaining bread flour 1 teaspoon at a time until dough is no longer sticky. Transfer to oiled bowl, turning to coat all surfaces. Cover bowl with damp towel. Let stand in warm draft-free area until doubled, about 1 to 1¹/₄ hours (an oven preheated to lowest setting for 2 minutes and then turned off works well; cushion bottom of bowl with pot holder).

Butter one 9 × 5-inch loaf pan and sprinkle with 2 tablespoons wheat germ. Transfer dough to lightly floured surface and roll into rectangle. Roll up lengthwise, pinching ends and seam tightly. Arrange loaf seam side down in prepared pan. Cover with damp towel. Let stand in warm draft-free area until almost doubled in volume, approximately 45 minutes.

Position rack in center of oven and preheat to 375°F. Brush top of loaf with glaze, being careful not to drip onto pan. Sprinkle loaf lightly with wheat germ. Bake until bread is golden brown and sounds hollow when tapped on bottom, covering lightly with aluminum foil if bread is browning too quickly, about 30 to 35 minutes. Remove bread from oven; invert onto wire rack and let cool completely before slicing.

Banana-Macadamia Nut Bread

Makes 1 loaf

- 3 large very ripe bananas
- 1 cup sugar
- ¹/₂ cup (1 stick) margarine, melted
- 2 cups sifted all purpose flour
- 1 teaspoon baking powder
- 1 teaspoon salt

- 2 eggs, beaten to blend
- 1 teaspoon baking soda dissolved in 1 tablespoon water
- ¹/₂ cup roasted salted macadamia nuts

Preheat oven to 350°F. Grease 9 × 5-inch loaf pan. Mash bananas in large bowl. Stir in sugar. Set aside 15 minutes. Beat in margarine using electric mixer. Combine flour, baking powder and salt in medium bowl. Blend into banana mixture in batches, mixing well after each addition. Add eggs and baking soda and mix well. Stir in nuts. Spoon into prepared pan, spreading evenly. Bake until bread is golden brown and tester inserted in center comes out clean, 60 to 65 minutes. Cool slightly and serve, or cool completely, wrap airtight and store at room temperature.

Serpentona

This pastry "snake" is filled with dried fruits and nuts for a spectacular holiday treat from Italy.

12 servings

Pastry
2¹/₃ cups all purpose flour
¹/₃ cup sugar
Pinch of salt
6 tablespoons vegetable oil
¹/₃ cup lukewarm water

Filling
3 tablespoons dark raisins
3 tablespoons golden raisins
6 tablespoons chopped walnuts
6 tablespoons slivered almonds
¹/₃ cup sugar

2 dried figs, quartered
2 pitted prunes, quartered
4 pitted dates, quartered
1 apple or pear, peeled, cored and coarsely chopped
¹/₄ cup semisweet chocolate chips
2 tablespoons dark rum or grappa*
1¹/₂ teaspoons grated orange peel
1 teaspoon grated lemon peel

1 egg yolk, beaten to blend (glaze)
2 small raisins
Sugar

For pastry: Combine flour, sugar and salt in processor. With machine running, pour oil and water through feed tube. Process just until dough binds together; do not form ball. Shape into disc. Wrap with plastic and let stand at room temperature for 30 minutes.

For filling: Cover raisins with hot water in small bowl. Let stand for 15 minutes. Drain and pat dry.

Combine drained raisins, walnuts, almonds, ¹/₃ cup sugar, figs, prunes and dates in processor. Chop coarsely, using on/off turns. Add apple and process until finely chopped using on/off turns. Transfer to bowl. Mix in chocolate, rum, orange and lemon peels.

Preheat oven to 350°F. Line baking sheet with parchment. Roll dough out on lightly floured surface to 13 × 24-inch oval. Spread filling on dough, leaving ¹/₂-inch border. Brush border with glaze. Roll dough up jelly roll fashion, starting at 1 long edge. Press edges and ends to seal. Squeeze roll 3 inches in from 1 end, forming snake head. Taper other end to form tail. Arrange pastry on prepared sheet, seam side down, coiling to resemble serpent. Brush with glaze. Press 2 raisins into head for "eyes." Sprinkle pastry with sugar. Bake until brown, about 1¹/₂ hours. Cool on rack before serving.

*Grappa is an Italian spirit available at specialty liquor stores.

Walnut Bread

Makes 1 loaf

2¹/₃ cups all purpose flour
1 tablespoon baking powder
¹/₂ teaspoon salt
1 cup minus 2 tablespoons milk

1 egg
³/₄ cup sugar
6 ounces walnuts, coarsely chopped

Preheat oven to 375°F. Butter and flour 9 × 5-inch loaf pan. Sift together flour, baking powder and salt. Whisk together milk and egg in large bowl. Whisk in sugar. Using wooden spoon, gradually stir in dry ingredients. Fold in walnuts. Turn batter into prepared pan. Bake until tester inserted in center comes out clean, about 50 minutes. Remove from pan. Cool bread completely on rack.

Penelope's Lemon Poppy Seed Bread

Makes one 4 × 7¹/₂-inch loaf

³/₄ cup sugar
2 eggs
¹/₂ cup milk
¹/₂ cup (1 stick) butter, melted and cooled
1 tablespoon lemon extract

1¹/₂ cups all purpose flour
1 teaspoon baking powder
1 teaspoon baking soda
¹/₂ teaspoon salt
3 tablespoons poppy seed

Preheat oven to 325°F. Grease and flour 4 × 7¹/₂-inch loaf pan. Combine sugar and eggs in large bowl and beat until very light and fluffy. Slowly beat in milk. Add butter and lemon extract and blend well.

Sift together flour, baking powder, baking soda and salt. Add to sugar mixture with poppy seed and stir to blend. Turn batter into prepared pan. Bake until bread is golden and tester inserted in center comes out clean, about 50 to 60 minutes. Remove from pan and let cool completely on rack.

Honey Coconut Loaf

Maks two 9 × 5-inch loaves

1¹/₄ cups honey
²/₃ cup sugar
¹/₂ cup water
3 eggs
¹/₃ cup oil
3¹/₂ cups rye flour

1¹/₄ cups flaked coconut
¹/₂ cup chopped citron
1 teaspoon baking soda
1 teaspoon salt
1 teaspoon cinnamon
¹/₂ teaspoon allspice

Preheat oven to 375°F. Grease two 9 × 5-inch loaf pans. Combine honey, sugar, water, eggs and oil in large bowl of electric mixer and blend well. Add all remaining ingredients and beat at medium speed 15 minutes. Pour batter evenly into prepared pans. Bake until tester inserted in centers comes out clean, about 55 to 60 minutes. Cool in pans 10 minutes, then turn out onto wire racks and let cool completely before slicing.

Apple and Currant Strudel

10 servings

Pastry
- 1/2 cup warm water
- 2 tablespoons vegetable oil
- 1 tablespoon sugar
- 2 cups all purpose flour
- 1 egg
- 1 egg white
- Vegetable oil

Filling
- 8 tart green apples
- 2 tablespoons fresh lemon juice

- Melted butter
- 1/2 cup currants

- 1/4 cup sugar
- 1/4 cup firmly packed light brown sugar
- Cinnamon
- Freshly grated nutmeg
- Grated lemon peel
- 1/2 cup ground toasted almonds

- Powdered sugar
- Whipped cream (optional)

For pastry: Blend water, 2 tablespoons oil and sugar in small bowl. Mound flour on work surface. Make well in center. Add water mixture, egg and white to well. Gradually draw flour from inner edge of well into center until all flour is incorporated. Gather dough into ball. Slap dough 100 times on counter to develop gluten. Rub dough with oil. Cover and let rest for 30 minutes.

For filling: Peel, core and thinly slice apples. Sprinkle with lemon juice.

To assemble: Oil baking sheet. Lightly oil hands. Set dough on 48-inch round table covered with floured cloth. Flatten dough into disc. Press dough into large circle. Begin stretching dough, pushing and pulling from center outward, until dough covers entire table; dough will be completely transparent. (Use floured cups to hold down edges of dough.) Cut off and discard thick edge of dough hanging over table.

Preheat oven to 425°F. Brush dough with butter. Arrange apple slices over 3/4 of dough. Sprinkle with currants and sugar. Dust with cinnamon, nutmeg and peel. Sprinkle almonds over covered and uncovered portions of dough. Using tablecloth as aid, roll dough up into log, tucking in ends.

Set strudel on prepared sheet, forming U shape. Brush with butter. Bake 15 minutes. Brush with butter. Reduce oven temperature to 350°F. Bake until golden brown, about 30 minutes. Cool slightly in pan. Cut into 2-inch pieces. Sprinkle lightly with powdered sugar. Serve with whipped cream if desired.

Sweet Easter Bread

Makes 2 large braids

- 1/4 cup warm water (105°F to 115°F)
- 2 tablespoons dry yeast

- 2/3 cup milk or fresh orange juice
- 2/3 cup sugar
- 10 tablespoons (1 1/4 sticks) butter
- 1/2 teaspoon salt
- 1 ounce Metaxa or other brandy

- 6 to 6 1/2 cups all purpose flour
- 2 teaspoons mahlepi,* crushed, or pinch of crushed aniseed and pinch of cinnamon

- 1 to 2 teaspoons cinnamon
- 1/2 teaspoon ground cardamom
- 4 eggs, well beaten

- 1 egg beaten with 1 tablespoon water
- Whole blanched almonds
- Sesame seed

Stir warm water and yeast in small bowl until yeast dissolves.

Heat milk in heavy medium saucepan. Stir in sugar, butter and salt until sugar dissolves and butter melts. Cool to 115°F. Blend in Metaxa.

Combine 6 cups flour, mahlepi, cinnamon and cardamom in bowl of heavy-duty mixer fitted with dough hook. Mix in yeast, milk mixture and 4 eggs at low speed until dough is well blended and just begins to cling to hook, about 3 minutes. (If dough seems too wet, beat in remaining flour 1 tablespoon at a time.) Continue mixing until dough clings to hook and cleans sides of bowl, about 5 minutes. Transfer to lightly floured surface and knead until smooth and elastic, 7 to 10 minutes. (Dough can also be prepared by hand or in processor.)

Butter large bowl. Add dough, turning to coat entire surface. Cover with plastic wrap or towel. Let dough rise in warm draft-free area until doubled in volume, about 1 hour.

Preheat oven to 350°F. Butter large baking sheet. Punch dough down. Turn out onto lightly floured surface and divide in half. Cut 1 portion into 3 equal pieces. Roll each piece into 16-inch-long rope 1½ inches thick. Braid ropes together. Repeat with remaining half. Place braids on prepared sheet. Pinch loose ends together and tuck under loaves. Let rise in warm draft-free area until doubled in volume.

Brush braids with some of egg glaze. Decorate with almonds. Brush almonds with egg glaze. Sprinkle with sesame seed. Bake until loaves are golden brown and sound hollow when tapped on bottom, about 40 minutes. (If tops brown too quickly, cover loosely with foil.) Cool completely. (*Can be prepared up to 2 days ahead, wrapped and stored at room temperature. Can also be prepared 1 month ahead and frozen. Thaw overnight in refrigerator.*)

*Ground seed of a wild, cherry-type fruit available at Middle Eastern or Greek markets.

Cinnamon Nut Wreath

12 servings

¼ cup dark raisins
¼ cup golden raisins
¼ cup brandy

Dough
1½ envelopes dry yeast
1 teaspoon sugar
¼ cup warm water (105°F to 115°F)

1 cup warm milk (105°F to 115°F)
¼ cup sugar
¼ cup (½ stick) unsalted butter, melted
1 teaspoon salt
2 eggs, room temperature, beaten to blend
4 cups (about) bread flour

Cinnamon Filling
½ cup sugar

½ cup firmly packed light brown sugar
½ cup ground almonds
½ cup finely chopped pecans
⅓ cup gingersnap or vanilla wafer crumbs
¼ cup shredded coconut
2 teaspoons cinnamon

¼ cup (½ stick) unsalted butter, room temperature

1 egg, beaten to blend
Lemon Glaze*
Candied cherries, pecan halves, blanched almonds and/or toasted coconut (garnishes)

Soak raisins in brandy in small bowl 3 hours, stirring occasionally.

For dough: Sprinkle yeast and 1 teaspoon sugar onto warm water in large bowl; stir to dissolve. Let stand until foamy, about 5 minutes.

Stir in milk, ¼ cup sugar, butter and salt. Blend in eggs. Add 2½ cups flour and mix until smooth. Add remaining flour ½ cup at a time until soft dough forms. Turn dough out onto lightly floured surface and knead until smooth and elastic, about 10 minutes, adding more flour if sticky. Grease large bowl. Add dough, turning to coat entire surface. Cover with plastic. Let dough rise in warm draft-free area until doubled, about 1 hour.

Punch dough down. Let rise again until doubled, about 45 minutes.

For filling: Combine both sugars, almonds, pecans, cookie crumbs, coconut and cinnamon in medium bowl.

Grease large edgeless baking sheet. Roll dough out on lightly floured surface to 12 × 18-inch rectangle. Spread butter over dough, leaving ½-inch border. Sprinkle filling over butter. Drain raisins and spread over filling. Roll dough up jelly roll fashion, starting at 1 long edge. Pinch seams to seal. Arrange in ring seam side down on prepared sheet. Pinch edges together to seal. Cut ¾ of the way through ring at 1¼-inch intervals, using serrated knife or scissors. Pull one section of wreath out and next one in all the way around. Let dough rise in warm draft-free area until almost doubled, about 45 minutes.

Preheat oven to 350°F. Brush wreath with egg. Bake until light brown, about 30 minutes. Transfer to rack and cool 15 minutes. Drizzle glaze over warm wreath. Top with garnishes. (*Wreath can be prepared 1 day ahead. Wrap tightly. Rewarm unwrapped in 350°F oven.*) Serve warm.

*Lemon Glaze

Makes about ½ cup

1½ cups powdered sugar	1 teaspoon fresh lemon juice
2½ tablespoons milk	1 teaspoon vanilla

Combine all ingredients in small bowl and mix until smooth.

Rum-Raisin Kugelhopf

If you do not have the traditional tall, narrow and decoratively fluted pan that is used in France, the standard bundt type will work just fine. This is also delicious sliced and toasted.

Makes 1

¾ cup golden raisins	1 teaspoon grated orange peel
2 tablespoons dark rum	¾ teaspoon salt
½ cup sugar	¾ cup (1½ sticks) unsalted butter, melted and cooled
1 envelope dry yeast	
¼ cup warm water (105°F to 115°F)	3 tablespoons unblanched sliced almonds
2½ cups bread flour	
3 eggs	

Combine raisins and rum in small plastic bag; seal. Soak raisins at least 2 hours, turning occasionally.

Grease large bowl. In small bowl, sprinkle 1 teaspoon sugar and yeast over water; stir to dissolve. Let stand until foamy, about 5 minutes.

Blend flour, remaining sugar, eggs, orange peel, salt and yeast mixture in processor for 5 seconds. With machine running, pour melted butter through feed tube and process until smooth batter forms, about 30 seconds. Transfer to prepared bowl. Cover bowl with oiled plastic. Let dough rise in warm draft-free area until tripled, about 3 hours.

Generously grease 12-cup kugelhopf pan or bundt pan and sprinkle with almonds. Stir raisin mixture into batter. Transfer to prepared pan. Cover pan. Let dough rise in warm draft-free area until doubled, about 2 hours.

Position rack in center of oven and preheat to 350°F. Bake kugelhopf until beginning to pull away from sides of pan, covering loosely with foil if top browns too quickly, about 40 minutes. Invert onto rack. Serve warm. (*Kugelhopf can be prepared 1 day ahead. Cool and wrap tightly. To reheat, uncover and place on baking sheet in cold oven. Set temperature at 300°F. Bake until warm, about 15 minutes.*)

Orange Apricot Braid

This elegant coffee cake, glossed with a clear, orange-apricot glaze and sprinkled with minced almonds, is surprisingly simple to make.

Makes 1

Dough

- 3 tablespoons sugar
- 1 envelope dry yeast
- 3 tablespoons warm water (105°F to 115°F)
- 3 cups bread flour
- ¼ cup (½ stick) unsalted butter, cut into 2 pieces, room temperature
- 1 egg
- 1 tablespoon grated orange peel
- ¾ teaspoon salt
- ½ cup milk

Apricot Filling and Glaze

- 35 dried apricots
- 1¼ cups sugar
- ½ cup fresh orange juice
- 1 egg
- 2 tablespoons minced unblanched almonds

For dough: Grease large bowl. In small bowl, sprinkle 1 teaspoon sugar and yeast over water; stir to dissolve. Let stand until foamy, about 5 minutes.

Blend flour, remaining sugar, butter, egg, orange peel, salt and yeast mixture in processor 5 seconds. With machine running, pour milk through feed tube and process until smooth, resilient dough forms, about 20 seconds. Transfer dough to prepared bowl, turning to coat entire surface. Cover and let rise in warm draft-free area until doubled, about 2 hours.

For filling and glaze: Heat 25 apricots, 1 cup sugar and orange juice in heavy 1-quart saucepan over low heat, swirling pan occasionally, until sugar dissolves. Increase heat and simmer until apricots are soft, about 7 minutes. Transfer apricots to work bowl, using slotted spoon. Boil cooking liquid until reduced to ½ cup. Reserve for glaze.

Process cooked apricots with steel knife 10 seconds. Add remaining ¼ cup sugar and egg and puree until smooth, about 10 seconds. Add remaining 10 apricots and finely chop, using on/off turns.

Grease large baking sheet. Roll dough out on generously floured surface to 12 × 15-inch rectangle. Trim edges. Transfer dough to prepared sheet. Spoon filling in 4-inch-wide strip down center of dough, leaving 1½-inch borders on 12-inch ends. Cut from edge of dough to edge of filling on each 12-inch end, 5½ inches in from each side to make flaps. Fold end flaps over filling. Make 9 diagonal cuts on each 15-inch side of dough, cutting from edge of filling to edge of dough and making strips. Trim out excess dough in four corners. Fold strips of dough to center, starting at upper end and overlapping alternate sides in center to form braid design and pressing edges to seal. Drape loosely with oiled plastic. Let rise in warm draft-free area until doubled, about 1 hour.

Position rack in center of oven and preheat to 350°F. Bake coffee cake until golden brown, about 30 minutes. Transfer to rack set over baking sheet. Rewarm glaze and brush over hot cake. Sprinkle cake with minced almonds. Serve warm.

Dresden Stollen

This is the perfect holiday bread, spiked with brandy and flecked with bits of candied fruits and nuts. Wrap up one loaf for giving and save one for breakfast.

Makes two 12-inch cakes

1/2 cup sugar
2 envelopes dry yeast
1/4 cup warm water (105°F to 115°F)
1 1/3 cups candied fruits
1/3 cup golden raisins
1/3 cup slivered almonds, toasted

3 cups bread flour
6 tablespoons (3/4 stick) unsalted butter, cut into 4 pieces, room temperature

2 egg yolks
1 egg
3/4 teaspoon salt
3/4 teaspoon freshly grated nutmeg
1/4 teaspoon mace
1/2 cup whipping cream
2 tablespoons brandy

1 tablespoon butter, melted
3 tablespoons powdered sugar

Sprinkle 1 teaspoon sugar and yeast over water in small bowl; stir to dissolve. Let stand until foamy, about 5 minutes. Combine candied fruits, raisins and almonds in large bowl.

Blend flour, remaining sugar, 6 tablespoons butter, yolks, egg, salt, nutmeg, mace and yeast mixture in processor 5 seconds. With machine running, pour cream and brandy through feed tube and process until smooth, resilient dough forms, about 20 seconds. Add to fruit. Knead in bowl to combine. Cover with towel and let rise in warm draft-free area until doubled in volume, about 2 hours.

Oil large baking sheet. Punch dough down and divide in half. Roll each piece out on generously floured surface to 10 × 7-inch oval with edges slightly thicker than center. Fold one long side over to 1/2 inch from opposite side. Transfer to prepared sheet, spacing 3 inches apart. Gently shape each loaf into crescent. Cover with oiled plastic. Let rise in warm draft-free area until doubled, about 1 1/4 hours.

Position rack in center of oven and preheat to 350°F. Brush stollens with melted butter. Bake until well browned, about 25 minutes. Transfer to racks and cool. Just before serving, dust with powdered sugar.

German Goese Ground Nut Stollen

Makes one 7 1/2-pound cake

1 3/4 cups golden raisins (1/2 pound)
1 3/4 cups dark currants (1/2 pound)
Flour

7 3/4 cups (2 pounds) plus 2 tablespoons all purpose flour
2 1/3 cups sugar (1 pound)
2 1/2 teaspoons baking powder
1/4 teaspoon *each* ground cardamom and mace
5 eggs
2 tablespoons dark rum
1/4 teaspoon *each* almond, lemon and vanilla extracts

2 cups ground hazelnuts (1/2 pound)
1 3/4 cups ground almonds (1/2 pound)
1 1/4 cups citron, diced
1 pound farmer's cheese (room temperature), cut into small pieces
1 1/2 cups (3 sticks) butter (room temperature), cut into small pieces

1 cup powdered sugar
3 tablespoons amaretto, Pernod, kirsch or dark rum

Grease large baking sheet. Combine raisins and currants in large mixing bowl and pour in enough boiling water to cover. Drain well; pat dry with paper towels. Coat fruits lightly with flour. Set aside.

Combine 7¾ cups flour, sugar, baking powder, cardamom and mace in large bowl and mix well. Add eggs, rum and extracts and blend well (mixture will be crumbly). Gather into ball. Transfer to large surface.

Preheat oven to 350°F. Spread mixture into flat oval shape. Cover with reserved raisins and currants and ground nuts. Coat citron lightly with flour. Sprinkle over ground nuts. Cover with pieces of cheese and butter.

Mix with hands until ingredients are blended, then knead until dough is smooth and elastic, about 7 to 10 minutes. Form dough into large baguette shape. Transfer to prepared baking sheet. Bake about 1½ hours. Let cool about 20 minutes on rack.

Combine powdered sugar and liqueur or rum in medium bowl. Brush over top of warm bread. Slice and serve.

Grossmutti's Coffee Cake

Makes 5 loaves

1½ packages dry yeast
¼ cup warm water (105°F to 115°F)
1¾ cups milk
½ cup (1 stick) butter
6¾ cups all purpose flour
1½ teaspoons salt
1½ cups raisins
1 cup plus 2 tablespoons sugar
2 eggs, beaten to blend

Topping
½ cup sugar
½ cup all purpose flour
¼ cup (½ stick) butter, room temperature
½ cup chopped walnuts

1 egg, beaten to blend

Cinnamon

Oil large bowl. Sprinkle yeast over warm water in another large bowl. Let stand until dissolved; stir to blend. Heat milk and butter in small saucepan over low heat until milk is warm (105°F to 115°F) and butter is soft but not completely melted, about 2 minutes. Blend into yeast mixture. Sift together flour and salt. Add 1 cup flour to yeast mixture. Blend in ½ cup raisins. Mix in 6 tablespoons sugar and ⅓ of 2 beaten eggs. Repeat twice. Blend in remaining flour. (Dough will be soft.) Transfer to prepared bowl and cover with towel. Let dough rise in warm draft-free area until doubled in volume, 3 to 4 hours.

For topping: Blend sugar, flour and butter in medium bowl with pastry blender or 2 knives until mixture is crumbly. Stir in chopped walnuts. Set aside.

Grease 2 baking sheets. Punch dough down. Divide into 5 pieces. (Dough will be sticky.) Form each piece into 6 × 4-inch oval. Transfer to prepared sheets. Brush loaves with beaten egg. Press half of topping onto tops of loaves. Cover with towels and let rise in warm draft-free area until almost doubled in volume, about 1½ hours.

Preheat oven to 275°F. Press remaining topping onto loaves. Sprinkle with cinnamon. Bake until lightly golden, about 40 minutes. Cool and wrap airtight. Store at room temperature, or freeze 1 month.

Almond Bundkuchen

Large and dramatic, this cake is perfect for a special brunch or breakfast.

16 servings

3/4 cup milk
1 cup golden raisins
1/2 cup currants

1 package dry yeast
1 teaspoon sugar
1/4 cup warm water (105°F to 115°F)

6 cups all purpose flour

1 cup (2 sticks) unsalted butter, room temperature
3/4 cup sugar

8 eggs, room temperature
2 tablespoons dark rum
1 1/2 tablespoons grated lemon peel
1/2 teaspoon salt

1/2 cup chopped toasted sliced almonds

3 tablespoons powdered sugar
3 tablespoons cinnamon

Scald milk in heavy medium saucepan. Stir in raisins and currants. Cool to warm (105°F to 115°F).

Sprinkle yeast and 1 teaspoon sugar over warm water in medium bowl; stir to dissolve. Let stand until foamy and proofed, about 5 minutes.

Strain cooled milk into yeast mixture, reserving fruit. Stir in 1 cup flour. Cover mixture and let rise in warm draft-free area until almost doubled in volume, about 30 minutes.

Cream butter with 3/4 cup sugar in large bowl of heavy-duty mixer fitted with dough hook until smooth. Beat in eggs 1 at a time and continue beating until mixture is light and fluffy. Mix in rum, lemon peel and salt. Blend in yeast mixture. Gradually add remaining flour and beat until smooth and satiny, about 1 minute. (Dough can also be prepared with standard electric mixer or by hand.) Stir in reserved golden raisins and currants.

Butter 10- to 12-cup tube or bundt pan. Spoon in half of dough. Sprinkle with almonds. Cover with remaining dough. Cover and let rise in warm draft-free area until dough comes to rim of pan, 1 to 1 1/2 hours.

Preheat oven to 350°F. Bake until cake is golden brown and sounds hollow when tapped on bottom, 50 to 60 minutes. Cool 5 minutes in pan. Invert onto rack and cool completely. Mix powdered sugar and cinnamon. Sprinkle over cake. (*Bundkuchen can be prepared several days ahead and refrigerated, or several weeks ahead and frozen.*)

Kasekuchen (Cheesecake with Streusel Topping)

16 servings

Pastry
1 cup all purpose flour
3 tablespoons sugar
1/4 teaspoon salt
1/2 cup (1 stick) unsalted butter
1 egg yolk

Filling
2 8-ounce packages cream cheese, room temperature
1 teaspoon vanilla

1/4 teaspoon salt
2 eggs, room temperature
1/2 cup sugar

Streusel Topping
1/3 cup all purpose flour
1/3 cup firmly packed light brown sugar
1/4 cup (1/2 stick) unsalted butter

For pastry: Preheat oven to 350°F. Sift together flour, sugar and salt into large bowl. Cut in butter using pastry blender or 2 knives until mixture resembles coarse meal. Add yolk and blend with fork until dough just comes together. Press into bottom and ½ inch up sides of 9-inch springform pan. Bake crust until golden brown, 20 to 25 minutes. Cool completely.

For filling: Preheat oven to 350°F. Using electric mixer, beat cream cheese, vanilla and salt in large bowl until fluffy. Using electric mixer, beat eggs and sugar in medium bowl until thick and light. Add to cream cheese mixture and beat until smooth. Spread evenly over crust. Bake until center is barely set, 35 minutes. Cool completely.

For topping: Preheat broiler. Combine flour and brown sugar in medium bowl. Cut in butter until mixture resembles coarse meal. Sprinkle over cheesecake. Broil 6 inches from heat until topping is browned and crisp, 2 to 3 minutes. Cool completely before serving. (*Can be prepared 2 days ahead and refrigerated. Bring cheesecake to room temperature before serving.*)

Golden Fruit and Vegetable Muffins

These moist muffins are reminiscent of a light fruitcake. They will keep for several days in an airtight container.

Makes 10 to 12

1½ cups all purpose flour
⅔ cup sugar
1 teaspoon ground coriander
1 teaspoon baking powder
½ teaspoon baking soda
½ teaspoon salt
¼ teaspoon freshly grated nutmeg
⅔ cup grated yellow straightneck squash

⅔ cup finely grated peeled carrot
⅓ cup finely chopped apricots
⅓ cup chopped golden raisins
2 eggs, room temperature
½ cup (1 stick) butter, melted and cooled
½ teaspoon vanilla

Preheat oven to 375°F. Generously grease 2½-inch muffin cups or line with paper baking cups. Mix first 7 ingredients in large bowl. Stir in squash, carrot, apricots and raisins. Whisk eggs in small bowl to blend. Whisk in butter and vanilla. Make well in center of dry ingredients. Add egg mixture to well; stir into dry ingredients until just blended (batter will be lumpy). Spoon batter into prepared cups, filling each ¾ full. Bake until muffins are golden brown and tester inserted in center comes out clean, about 30 minutes. Cool 5 minutes. Turn out of pan. Serve warm or at room temperature.

Double Fudge Muffins

Dense and rich, these are for true brownie lovers.

Makes about 16

5 ounces semisweet chocolate, coarsely chopped
2 ounces unsweetened chocolate, coarsely chopped
⅓ cup butter
¾ cup sour cream
⅔ cup firmly packed brown sugar
¼ cup light corn syrup

1 egg, room temperature
1¼ teaspoons vanilla
1½ cups all purpose flour
1 teaspoon baking soda
¼ teaspoon salt
5 ounces semisweet chocolate, cut into ⅓-inch pieces or 1 cup semisweet chocolate chips

Preheat oven to 400°F. Generously grease 2½-inch muffin cups or line with foil baking cups. Melt first 3 ingredients in medium bowl set over saucepan of barely simmering water. Stir until smooth. Cool slightly.

Whisk sour cream, sugar, corn syrup, egg and vanilla into chocolate. Mix flour, baking soda and salt in large bowl. Mix in 1 cup chopped chocolate. Make well in center of dry ingredients. Add chocolate mixture to well; stir into dry ingredients until just blended (batter will be lumpy). Spoon batter into prepared cups, filling each ³/4 full. Bake muffins until tester inserted in center comes out moist and almost clean, about 20 minutes. Cool 5 minutes. Serve warm.

Jumbo Ginger Breadmen

You can give one of these charming breads to each member of the family on Christmas morning. Tie a wide silken red ribbon around the center and attach a gift card. To serve, pass a crock of sweet butter or orange marmalade. Excellent with cinnamon-spiked hot chocolate.

Makes 6

1¹/2 cups milk
10 tablespoons (1¹/4 sticks) unsalted butter
²/3 cup unsulphured molasses
¹/3 cup finely minced crystallized ginger
3¹/4 teaspoons ground ginger
1 tablespoon grated orange peel
1 tablespoon ground coriander
2 teaspoons cinnamon
1¹/4 teaspoons salt
1 teaspoon ground cloves
1 teaspoon mace

2 envelopes dry yeast
¹/3 cup warm water (105°F to 115°F)
1 tablespoon unsulphured molasses

2 eggs
1¹/2 cups graham or whole wheat flour
6 cups (about) unbleached all purpose flour

12 whole allspice
6 red candied cherry halves
18 blanched almonds
1 egg beaten with 1 tablespoon milk (glaze)

Heat milk with butter in heavy small saucepan over low heat until milk is scalded and butter melts. Remove from heat and stir in ²/3 cup molasses, crystallized ginger, ground ginger, orange peel, coriander, cinnamon, salt, cloves and mace. Let stand 1 hour.

Sprinkle yeast over ¹/3 cup warm water in bowl of heavy-duty electric mixer. Add 1 tablespoon molasses and stir to dissolve yeast. Cover and let stand until foamy, about 5 minutes.

Blend milk mixture into yeast, using dough hook. Add eggs 1 at a time, mixing until well combined. Blend in graham flour. Add enough all purpose flour 1 cup at a time to form elastic dough that pulls away from sides of bowl. Knead until very smooth and no longer sticky, at least 5 minutes. (*Bread can also be made by hand.*)

Transfer dough to large buttered bowl, turning to coat entire surface. Cover bowl with plastic and kitchen towel. (*Can be prepared 1 day ahead and refrigerated. Let rise in refrigerator until doubled. Punch down when doubled and cover tightly.*) Let dough rise in warm draft-free area until just doubled in volume, about 1¹/2 hours for room temperature dough or 3 hours for chilled.

Line baking sheets with buttered parchment. Punch dough down. Divide into 6 pieces. Pinch ¹/4 off 1 piece to use for head. Form larger piece into oval. Flatten lightly with rolling pin to 7-inch-long oval. To form arms, start ¹/3 down from top of oval on right side and cut diagonally ¹/2 way to center of oval. Repeat on left side. Cut center of oval ¹/3 up from bottom to form legs. Transfer to prepared sheet. Swing arms away from body; flatten slightly. Press ends to form round, fat hands. Separate legs and flatten slightly. Press ends to form round feet. Roll reserved small piece of dough into ball. Flatten slightly to form head. Moisten 1 end and attach to body, overlapping slightly at neck. Form 5 more men with remaining dough pieces.

Press 2 allspice in center of each head for eyes. Press cherry half below eyes for mouth. Press 3 almonds down front for buttons. Brush each ginger breadman with egg-milk glaze.

Preheat oven to 350°F. Let bread rise for 15 minutes while oven is heating.

Bake bread until rich golden brown, 20 to 25 minutes. Cool on racks. (*Can be prepared 1 day ahead. Cool completely. Wrap airtight. Reheat in 350°F oven 5 to 10 minutes.*) Serve warm.

❧ *Cakes and Cookies*

Old World Sour Cream Pound Cake

8 to 10 servings

1 cup (2 sticks) butter, room temperature	1/2 teaspoon salt
2³/4 cups sugar	1/4 teaspoon baking soda
6 eggs, room temperature	1¹/4 cups sour cream
3 cups sifted all purpose flour	1 teaspoon vanilla

Preheat oven to 350°F. Grease and flour 10-inch tube pan. Cream butter with sugar using electric mixer. Add eggs one at a time, beating well after each addition. Sift flour with salt and baking soda. Add flour to butter mixture in three batches alternately with sour cream, mixing well after each addition. Blend in vanilla. Pour batter into prepared pan. Bake until top is light brown and tester inserted near center comes out clean, about 1¹/4 hours. Cool cake completely in pan before serving.

Dried Apple and Molasses Cake

Makes 1 loaf

1 cup dried apples	1/2 teaspoon freshly grated nutmeg
³/4 cup dark molasses	1/2 teaspoon salt
1/2 cup chopped walnuts	1 cup sugar
	1/2 cup sour cream
2 cups all purpose flour	1 egg
2 teaspoons baking soda	Whipped cream or
1 teaspoon cinnamon	vanilla ice cream
1/2 teaspoon ground cloves	

Soak 1 cup dried apples overnight in enough water to cover.

Drain apples; pat completely dry. Chop finely. Combine apples and molasses in heavy small saucepan. Cover and simmer 20 minutes. Let cool to room temperature. Stir in walnuts.

Preheat oven to 350°F. Butter 9 × 5-inch loaf pan. Line with waxed paper; butter and flour paper. Sift flour, baking soda, cinnamon, cloves, nutmeg and salt. Whisk sugar, sour cream and egg in large bowl until thick and smooth. Gradually stir dry ingredients into sugar mixture. Stir in apple mixture. Pour batter into prepared pan, smoothing top. Bake until tester inserted in center comes out clean, about 1 hour. Invert cake onto rack and cool completely. Cut into thin slices. Serve with whipped cream or ice cream. (*Apple cake can be prepared one month ahead, wrapped and frozen.*)

Grandmother's Gingerbread

10 servings

¹/₂ cup solid vegetable shortening
1 cup light molasses
1 cup sugar
2 eggs beaten
2 cups all purpose flour
1 teaspoon salt
1 teaspoon ground cloves
1 teaspoon freshly grated nutmeg

2 teaspoons cinnamon
2 teaspoons ground ginger
1 cup boiling water
1 teaspoon baking soda

Whipped cream or vanilla ice cream

Preheat oven to 350°F. Grease 9 × 11-inch baking pan. Combine all ingredients except boiling water, baking soda and garnish in large bowl *in order given*, mixing well after each addition. Combine boiling water and baking soda in small bowl and stir until dissolved. Blend into molasses mixture.

Pour batter into prepared pan. Bake until tester inserted in center comes out clean, about 45 minutes. Cool slightly. Cut into squares. Serve gingerbread warm with whipped cream or vanilla ice cream.

Easy Apricot Cake

Bake this cake 1 or 2 days before serving to allow flavors to intensify. It keeps well one week in the refrigerator.

12 servings

2 cups self-rising flour (or 2 cups all purpose flour sifted with 1 teaspoon baking powder and ¹/₂ teaspoon salt)
2 cups sugar
1 cup corn oil
2 small jars strained apricot baby food
3 eggs
2 teaspoons vanilla
1 teaspoon cinnamon
¹/₂ teaspoon cloves

¹/₂ cup apricot jam

Frosting
3 cups powdered sugar
3 tablespoons margarine, room temperature
3 tablespoons half and half
1 tablespoon bourbon

Preheat oven to 350°F. Grease a 3-quart rectangular casserole or 2 9-inch square baking pans. Combine first 8 ingredients in large bowl and mix thoroughly. Turn into baking pans and bake until tester inserted in center comes out clean, 30 to 35 minutes. Let cool.

Remove cake from pans. If baked in 1 rectangular pan, cut in half lengthwise. Place bottom layer on platter and spread with jam. Top with second layer.

Combine ingredients for frosting in small bowl and mix to spreading consistency. Frost top and sides of cake. Refrigerate until ready to slice and serve.

Honey Cake

Makes 1 loaf

1 cup honey
1 cup *unpacked* brown sugar
2 eggs
1/2 cup vegetable oil
1/2 cup coffee
1/8 teaspoon baking soda
Pinch of salt

3 cups rye flour
Pinch of cloves
Pinch of allspice
Pinch of cinnamon
1/2 cup coarsely chopped walnuts, toasted

Preheat oven to 325°F. Grease and flour 9 × 5-inch loaf pan. Blend first 7 ingredients about 2 minutes with mixer at low speed. Add remaining ingredients except walnuts and mix on medium speed until smooth, about 5 minutes. Blend in nuts. Turn into loaf pan and bake until toothpick inserted in center comes out clean, about 1 1/2 hours. Cool 10 minutes. Remove from pan and cool completely on wire rack.

Sesame Streusel Cake

The sesame flavor comes from three sources: tahini, sesame oil and toasted whole seeds. Since this loaf is not very sweet, it is perfect for breakfast.

Makes 1 loaf

Batter
1/2 cup (1 stick) butter, room temperature
1/2 cup tahini (sesame seed paste)*
1 1/2 teaspoons sesame oil
1 cup sugar
4 eggs, room temperature
2 teaspoons vanilla
2 cups all purpose flour
1 teaspoon baking powder
1/2 teaspoon salt
1/2 cup milk
3 tablespoons toasted sesame seed

Streusel
1/4 cup firmly packed light brown sugar
1/4 cup all purpose flour
2 tablespoons (1/4 stick) butter, room temperature
1 tablespoon tahini
1/2 teaspoon cinnamon

2 teaspoons toasted sesame seed

For batter: Preheat oven to 325°F. Butter and flour 9 × 5-inch loaf pan. Cream 1/2 cup butter, tahini and sesame oil in large bowl of electric mixer until fluffy. Gradually beat in sugar. Beat in eggs one at a time. Blend in vanilla. Sift in flour, baking powder and salt alternately with milk, stirring gently with wooden spoon until just blended; do not overmix. Fold in 3 tablespoons toasted sesame seed.

For streusel: Blend brown sugar, flour, butter, tahini and cinnamon in small bowl with fork or pastry blender until mixture is very crumbly.

Turn batter into prepared pan, spreading slightly higher at sides. Sprinkle evenly with streusel. Top with 2 teaspoons sesame seed. Bake until tester inserted in center comes out clean, about 1 1/4 hours. Cool cake in pan. (*This cake will keep, wrapped tightly, 1 week at room temperature or several weeks in the refrigerator. It can also be frozen.*)

*Available at natural foods stores.

Plum Pudding

These traditional holiday desserts can be made in coffee cans if you don't have pudding molds, and the cans are fun to give as gifts when decorated.

Makes 4 puddings

1 cup all purpose flour
2 cups finely minced suet
³/₄ cup plus 2 tablespoons currants
1¹/₂ cups dark raisins
1 cup golden raisins
1 pippin apple, peeled, cored and finely chopped
1 teaspoon ground allspice
1¹/₄ cups chopped prunes
1¹/₂ cups breadcrumbs
1¹/₂ cups firmly packed brown sugar
¹/₂ cup candied fruit or fruitcake mix
¹/₂ teaspoon salt

¹/₂ teaspoon ground cloves
¹/₂ teaspoon mace
¹/₂ lemon, unpeeled and finely chopped
1 orange, unpeeled and finely chopped
3 eggs
6 tablespoons rum
¹/₂ cup beer

Brandy

Preheat oven to 325°F. Butter four 3-cup pudding molds. Combine all ingredients in order listed in large mixing bowl and blend well. Fill prepared molds ²/₃ full with pudding mixture, packing tightly. Cover or seal molds with aluminum foil. Invert four small glass custard cups in center of large deep pan. Set molds on top of cups. Fill pan with boiling water. Place additional pan of water in bottom of oven. Steam until tops begin to brown and centers of puddings feel firm to touch, about 3 to 3¹/₂ hours, checking level of water in pan occasionally and adding more boiling water if necessary.

Let puddings cool. Run sharp knife around edges of molds. Moisten 4 large pieces of cheesecloth with brandy. Unmold puddings; wrap with cloths. Cover each with plastic wrap, then foil. Chill.

English Plum Pudding

10 to 12 servings

³/₄ cup brandy (or more)
¹/₄ pound beef suet, ground
2¹/₂ cups fresh fine breadcrumbs
1¹/₄ cups firmly packed light brown sugar
1¹/₄ cups golden raisins
1¹/₄ cups dark raisins
1¹/₄ cups currants
³/₄ cup glacéed cherries
³/₄ cup slivered almonds
¹/₂ cup glacéed lemon peel
¹/₂ cup glacéed orange peel
¹/₂ cup all purpose flour
2 eggs, beaten to blend

1 small tart green apple, peeled, cored and grated
Grated peel of 1 orange
3 tablespoons molasses
1 teaspoon allspice
1 teaspoon cinnamon
1 teaspoon baking soda
¹/₂ teaspoon cloves
¹/₂ teaspoon salt
¹/₄ teaspoon freshly grated nutmeg

Holly sprig (garnish)
Hard Sauce*

Butter 2-quart pudding mold. Add water to large steamer to within 1 inch of rack. Cover and bring to boil over medium-high heat (do not let boiling water touch rack). Meanwhile, combine ¹/₂ cup brandy with all remaining ingredients (except garnish and sauce) in large bowl and mix thoroughly. Turn mixture into prepared mold. Cover with foil and tie tightly with string. Reduce heat to medium-low, carefully remove steamer cover and set mold on rack. Cover and steam 4 hours, adding water occasionally to steamer as necessary. Store at room temperature at least 3 months, adding drops of brandy or rum to pudding about once a week to moisten.

To serve, resteam pudding in same manner 1 hour. Invert pudding onto rimmed serving dish. Heat remaining ¼ cup brandy in small saucepan. Pour over pudding and ignite. Garnish with holly sprig. Pass sauce separately.

*Hard Sauce

Makes about 1 cup

½ cup (1 stick) unsalted butter, room temperature
½ cup powdered sugar

⅛ teaspoon freshly grated nutmeg
2 tablespoons dark rum or brandy
1 teaspoon vanilla

Cream butter in medium bowl. Beat in powdered sugar and nutmeg. Blend in rum and vanilla. Chill until firm.

Christmas Fruitcake Soufflé

Makes 5 cakes

1 pound pitted dates
1 pound dried apricot halves
½ pound Brazil nuts
½ pound walnut halves
½ pound pecan halves
1 cup diced glacéed fruit
1 cup drained maraschino cherries
3 ounces glacéed apricots, halved
1½ cups all purpose flour
1 teaspoon baking powder

1½ cups sugar
6 eggs, room temperature
2 teaspoons vanilla
1 teaspoon salt
Glacéed cherries and nuts (garnish)

1¼ cups brandy

Preheat oven to 300°F. Cut circles of waxed paper to fit bottoms of five 2-cup soufflé dishes. Grease each dish well and fit with foil collars. Combine first 8 ingredients in large bowl. Sift flour and baking powder over top. Stir until mixture is well coated. Combine sugar, eggs, vanilla and salt in medium bowl and beat until slightly foamy. Pour egg mixture over fruit and nuts and blend gently. Divide evenly among prepared dishes. Lightly press mixture down into dishes. Garnish tops with cherries and nuts. Bake until tester inserted in centers comes out clean, 1¼ hours.

Remove from oven and immediately drizzle each cake with 2 tablespoons brandy. Let cool. Discard foil collars. Remove cakes from dishes. Wash and dry dishes. Replace cakes. Drizzle each cake with 2 tablespoons brandy. When completely cool, wrap each cake in plastic, colored tissue and ribbon.

Gateau Breton

Makes 1 loaf

¾ cup prune juice
9 pitted prunes (3½ ounces), coarsely chopped
½ teaspoon grated orange peel

1 cup (2 sticks) butter, room temperature

1⅓ cups sugar
1 tablespoon grated orange peel
5 eggs, room temperature
1¾ cups all purpose flour
2 teaspoons orange flower water

Bring prune juice, prunes and orange peel to simmer in heavy small saucepan over medium heat. Reduce heat to low and simmer until mixture is reduced to stiff paste, stirring frequently toward end of cooking time to mash prunes and prevent burning. Set aside and let cool completely.

Preheat oven to 300°F. Butter and flour 9 × 5-inch loaf pan. Cream 1 cup butter in large bowl of electric mixer until fluffy. Gradually beat in sugar. Blend in orange peel. Beat in 4 eggs one at a time. Sift in flour. Stir in remaining egg with orange flower water.

Spread ⅔ of batter in prepared pan. Top with prune mixture, leaving ½-inch border at edges. Spread remaining batter over. Bake until cake is deep golden and tester inserted in center comes out clean, about 1 hour and 40 minutes. Cool cake in pan on rack. (*Gateau Breton will keep, wrapped tightly, for 1 week at room temperature or several weeks if refrigerated. It can also be frozen.*)

Fudge Chip Pound Cake

Makes 1 loaf

6 tablespoons sugar
3 tablespoons unsweetened cocoa powder, sifted
1½ tablespoons water

½ cup (1 stick) butter, room temperature
1 cup sugar
2 eggs, room temperature
1 teaspoon vanilla

1½ cups all purpose flour
1 teaspoon baking powder
¼ teaspoon salt
½ cup milk
½ cup semisweet chocolate chips

⅛ teaspoon baking soda

Blend sugar and cocoa in heavy small saucepan. Stir in water. Bring to simmer over medium-low heat, stirring until smooth. Simmer mixture gently 3 minutes. Cool completely.

Preheat oven to 350°F. Butter and flour 9 × 5-inch loaf pan. Cream ½ cup butter in large bowl of electric mixer until fluffy. Gradually beat in sugar. Beat in eggs one at a time. Blend in vanilla. Sift flour with baking powder and salt. Add flour mixture to batter alternately with milk, blending well after each addition. Fold in chocolate chips.

Turn ⅓ of batter into prepared pan, spreading higher at edges. Divide remaining batter in half. Blend half into cooled cocoa mixture with baking soda. Spoon over batter in pan and spread, leaving ½-inch border at edges. Top with remaining light batter. Bake until tester inserted in center comes out clean, 65 to 70 minutes. Cool in pan 10 minutes. Invert cake onto rack and cool completely. (*The cake will stay moist, wrapped tightly, for 1 week at room temperature or several weeks in the refrigerator. It can also be frozen.*)

Scotch Bun

The impressive appearance of this "bun"—really a dense fruitcake encased in pastry—is an event in itself.

16 servings

Pastry
- 3¹/₃ cups all purpose flour, sifted
- ¹/₄ teaspoon salt
- 1 cup (2 sticks) unsalted butter, cut into small pieces
- 2 egg yolks
- 6 tablespoons cold water
- 2 tablespoons vegetable oil

Batter
- 4 cups raisins, chopped (1¹/₂ pounds)
- 4 cups dried currants (about 1 pound)
- 1 cup slivered almonds
- 1 cup sugar
- 1 cup diced mixed candied fruit peel (4 ounces)
- 2 cups all purpose flour
- 2 teaspoons cinnamon
- 2 teaspoons ginger
- 2 teaspoons freshly grated nutmeg
- 1 teaspoon allspice
- 1 teaspoon baking soda
- 1 teaspoon cream of tartar
- ¹/₂ teaspoon freshly ground pepper
- ¹/₂ teaspoon cloves
- ¹/₄ teaspoon salt
- 1¹/₂ cups buttermilk
- ³/₄ cup Cognac
- 4 eggs, beaten to blend

- 1 egg yolk, beaten with 1 tablespoon cold water
- 1 tablespoon Cognac (optional)

For pastry: Mix flour and salt in large bowl. Cut in butter with pastry blender until mixture resembles coarse meal. Blend yolks with cold water and oil. Add to flour and mix with fork. Pat dough into ball. Flatten slightly and dust with flour. Wrap dough tightly in plastic. Chill at least 1 hour.

For batter: Preheat oven to 350°F (or 325°F for glass dish). Combine raisins, currants, almonds, sugar and candied peel in large bowl. Sift together flour, cinnamon, ginger, nutmeg, allspice, baking soda, cream of tartar, pepper, cloves and salt. Resift flour mixture over dried fruit and nuts and toss gently to blend. Add buttermilk, ³/₄ cup Cognac and eggs and mix well.

Roll ²/₃ of dough out on lightly floured surface to fit 2¹/₂-quart mold or glass baking dish, allowing ¹/₄-inch overhang. Transfer to mold. Roll remaining dough out to fit over top. Turn batter into pastry shell. Moisten edges of pastry in mold. Cover filling with remaining piece of pastry; trim and crimp edges with fork to seal. Prick top with fork. Poke skewer through pastry and filling in several places to allow steam to escape. Bake 30 minutes. Reduce oven temperature to 300°F (or 275°F for glass dish) and continue baking 3 hours, brushing top with egg mixture after 2¹/₂ hours; crust will be golden brown after about 1 hour. Remove from oven. Brush top with Cognac if desired. Set aside 3 to 4 days before serving.

Apricot-Macadamia Nut Fruitcake

A cup of hot apricot tea is the perfect accompaniment to this tropical fruitcake.

8 to 10 servings

- ³/₄ cup (1¹/₂ sticks) butter
- 1 cup sugar
- 3 eggs, separated
- ¹/₂ cup milk
- 2 tablespoons apricot brandy
- ¹/₂ teaspoon vanilla
- 1³/₄ cups sifted all purpose flour
- 1 cup chopped dried apricots
- 1 cup golden raisins
- 1 cup chopped roasted and salted macadamia nuts
- ¹/₄ teaspoon cream of tartar

Preheat oven to 275°F. Grease and flour 6-cup bundt pan. Cream butter with sugar in large bowl of electric mixer. Beat yolks to blend in small bowl and add to butter mixture. Combine milk, brandy and vanilla in another small bowl. Add

Almond-Walnut Butter Toffee

From left: Bittersweet Chocolate Caramels with Burnt Almonds; Red Onion and Rosemary Marmalade with Cassis; Roasted Red Pepper Mustard; Jumbo Ginger Breadmen; Nürnberger Lebkuchen Bars with Lemon Glaze; Apricots in Rum with Ginger and Sultanas; Olive Oil Flavored with Porcini Mushrooms, Garlic and Herbs

Clockwise from top: Caramelized Orange Sections; Marzipan Fruit; Caramel Moux; Marzipan Animals; Nougat Montelimar surrounded by Chocolate-covered Brandied Cherries; silver tray of Peanut Butter Feuilleté and Gianduja "Bacon"; center: silver dish of Coconut Snowballs and plate of Branche surrounded by Deluxe Holiday Mints

Sage Cheddar Breadsticks and Hickory-Smoked Cheddar Crackers

Brian Leatart

Clockwise from top left: Christmas Fruit-cake Soufflé; Sweet Yellow Squash Pickles; Windmill Cookies; Brown Sugar Pecan Brownies; English Plum Pudding

Alan Krosnick

Brian Leatart

Top right, boxed: Toasted Coconut Marshmallows; center: small plate of Fruit and Nut Rolls and dish of Sunflower Seed Brittle; bottom: Old-Fashioned Peanut Brittle

Merry Christmas

to butter alternately with flour in 4 batches, mixing well after each addition. Stir in apricots, raisins and nuts. Beat whites until soft peaks form. Add cream of tartar and continue beating until stiff but not dry. Gently fold whites into batter. Spoon into prepared pan, spreading evenly. Bake until tester inserted in center comes out clean, about 2¼ hours. Cool completely in pan on rack. Slice and serve; or wrap airtight with plastic and store at room temperature.

Guinness English Fruitcake

An unusual cake spiked with the distinct flavor of the frothy stout. For an elegant offering, wrap it in clear cellophane tied with a green ribbon and present it in a basket with several bottles of Guinness and a cake knife.

Makes one 9-inch cake

1½ cups (3 sticks) unsalted butter, softened
1½ cups firmly packed dark brown sugar
½ cup treacle*
5 eggs
4½ cups all purpose flour, sifted
1½ teaspoons baking soda
1 teaspoon salt
1 teaspoon cinnamon
1 teaspoon ground allspice
1 teaspoon ground cardamom
½ teaspoon ground cloves
1 cup coarsely chopped English black walnuts

⅔ cup snipped dates
⅔ cup coarsely chopped pitted prunes
⅓ cup dried currants
⅓ cup raisins
⅓ cup coarsely diced candied citron
⅓ cup coarsely diced candied orange peel
1 tablespoon grated orange peel
1 tablespoon grated lemon peel
10 ounces (1¼ cups) Guinness stout, opened 1 hour, room temperature

Additional stout
Whipped cream

Position rack in center of oven and preheat to 325°F. Butter 9-inch springform pan (with 3-inch sides). Line bottom of pan with parchment. Line sides of pan with 5-inch band of parchment (paper should come 2 inches over rim), overlapping to seal. Butter paper. Using electric mixer, cream 1½ cups butter and sugar until light and fluffy. Gradually beat in treacle. Beat in eggs 1 at a time. Sift together flour, baking soda, salt and spices. Add to creamed mixture 1 cup at a time, mixing until smooth. Beat in remaining ingredients except stout and whipped cream. Add enough stout (about ¾ cup) to bind all ingredients (batter should be heavy, sticky and spreadable). Turn batter into prepared pan, smoothing top. Bake cake 1 hour.

Reduce oven to 300°F and continue baking until tester inserted in center comes out clean and cake pulls away from sides of pan, about 1 hour (if top browns too quickly, cover loosely with foil). Cool cake slightly in pan on rack. Remove springform. Peel off parchment. Pierce cake all over using skewer. Brush with remaining ½ cup stout. Wrap tightly and store in airtight container up to 1 week, brushing with additional stout every other day. To serve, cut cake into thin slices and top with whipped cream.

*A thick, dark syrup available at specialty foods stores. If unavailable, use molasses.

Date Cake

Prepare this delicious cake a week ahead. Wrap it in a colorful canister or basket for gift giving. It also packs well for mailing.

18 to 20 servings

³/₄ cup (1¹/₂ sticks) butter
1¹/₂ cups firmly packed dark brown sugar
1 pound dates, pitted and coarsely chopped
1 cup all purpose flour
1 cup walnuts, chopped
2 eggs, beaten
¹/₂ teaspoon salt
1 cup boiling water
1 teaspoon baking soda
2 tablespoons dark rum

Frosting
1¹/₂ cups powdered sugar
³/₄ cup (1¹/₂ sticks) butter, room temperature
2¹/₂ tablespoons dark rum

Preheat oven to 350°F. Line bottom of 10-inch tube pan with parchment paper; butter paper. Cream ³/₄ cup butter with brown sugar in large bowl until light and fluffy. Blend in dates, flour, walnuts, eggs and salt. Combine 1 cup boiling water with baking soda in small bowl. Pour into batter, blending well. Transfer to prepared pan. Bake until tester inserted near center comes out clean, about 1 hour. Pour 2 tablespoons rum over top. Let stand until outside of pan is cool. Invert cake onto platter and cool.

For frosting: Combine sugar, butter and rum in medium bowl and mix until well blended. Spread over top and sides of cake. Refrigerate until ready to serve.

Mother's Fruitcake

Makes 4 cakes

2 pounds dates, coarsely chopped
2 pounds pecans, coarsely chopped
1 pound candied cherries, coarsely chopped
1 pound candied pineapple, coarsely chopped

2 cups all purpose flour
2 cups sugar
8 eggs
2 teaspoons baking powder

Preheat oven to 300°F. Line four 7 × 2¹/₄-inch loaf pans with parchment paper; grease paper. Combine dates, pecans and candied fruit in large bowl and mix well. Add 1 cup flour and toss to coat. Combine sugar and eggs in another large bowl and blend until smooth. Stir in remaining flour and baking powder and mix well. Add to fruit mixture and blend well. Pack mixture evenly into prepared pans. Place pan filled with water in bottom of oven. Set loaves on rack above. Bake until tester inserted in center comes out clean, about 2 hours (cakes will be moist). Let cool completely. Turn cakes out of pans. Cover with plastic wrap or aluminum foil. Store in cool, dark place. (*Fruitcakes can be frozen.*)

The Four Seasons Fruitcake

This elegant, marzipan-wrapped cake comes from New York's famous The Four Seasons.

Makes six 8 × 4-inch fruitcakes

1 pound 10 ounces (6½ sticks) unsalted butter, room temperature
1 pound 10 ounces sugar (about 3½ cups)
20 eggs
2 pounds 12 ounces bread flour (about 11 cups)

3 pounds candied fruit (oranges, lemons, angelica, red and green cherries), chopped
1 vanilla bean
½ cup rum
½ teaspoon ground cinnamon
½ teaspoon ground ginger

Grated peel of 2 lemons
Juice of 1 lemon

2 cups coarsely chopped walnuts

Topping
Powdered sugar
3 pounds Marzipan* (about 6 cups)

½ cup Simple Syrup**

Granulated sugar
Melted semisweet chocolate and chocolate leaves (optional)

Grease and flour 6 8 × 4 × 2½-inch loaf pans. Preheat oven to 400°F. Cream butter in large mixing bowl until smooth. Gradually add sugar and beat until very light and fluffy. Begin adding eggs 3 at a time, beating well after each addition. When 9 eggs have been added, beat in about ½ pound flour. Add remaining eggs a few at a time.

Add about 1 cup flour to fruit and toss to coat. Stir remaining flour into egg mixture. Split vanilla bean lengthwise and scrape seeds into batter. Blend in rum, spices, lemon peel and juice.

Add fruit mixture and nuts and stir just to mix. Divide among prepared pans, tapping each against work surface to settle mixture. Smooth top with spatula. Set pans on baking sheet and bake about 1¼ hours, checking frequently toward end of cooking time to prevent burning. Let cool completely.

For topping: Sprinkle work surface with powdered sugar. Divide marzipan into 5 parts. Roll each into rectangle ¼ inch thick, sprinkling with additional sugar as necessary to prevent sticking. Trim each to 8 × 14-inch rectangle.

Brush each rectangle with syrup. Turn fruitcakes out of pans; if tops of any cakes are rounded, trim so they are flat. Set on marzipan rectangles and roll each to cover completely; trim marzipan at ends if necessary to make neat package.

Sprinkle some granulated sugar on sheet of waxed paper. Brush top and sides of cakes with syrup and then dip in sugar to coat. Using thin sharp knife, make cross-hatch design on top. Decorate sides with stripe of melted chocolate and top with chocolate leaves.

*Marzipan

Makes 3 pounds

6 cups almond paste
4 cups powdered sugar

6 egg whites

Combine all ingredients in large bowl of electric mixer and blend well.

**Simple Syrup

½ cup water
¼ cup sugar

Combine water and sugar in small saucepan. Bring to boil over medium heat, stirring just until sugar is dissolved, and let boil 5 minutes. Cool completely before using.

Certosino (Fruitcake from Bologna)

Serve this with dessert wine or a bottle of chilled Asti Spumante.

12 servings

½ cup golden raisins
¾ cup Marsala

⅔ cup candied citron
⅓ cup candied cherries
⅔ cup blanched almonds, coarsely chopped
½ cup pine nuts
2 ounces semisweet chocolate, coarsely chopped
1 teaspoon cinnamon
1 teaspoon aniseed

1 cup honey
¾ cup sugar
3 tablespoons butter
2 cups all purpose flour
2 teaspoons baking soda
⅓ cup whole blanched almonds

Soak golden raisins in Marsala for 20 minutes, stirring occasionally.

Preheat oven to 350°F. Butter 10-inch springform pan. Coarsely chop citron and cherries. Set aside ⅓ cup mixture for decoration. Combine remainder with ⅔ cup almonds, pine nuts, chocolate, cinnamon and aniseed. Drain raisins, reserving Marsala; add raisins to fruit and nut mixture.

Heat honey, sugar, butter and reserved Marsala in heavy large saucepan over low heat, swirling pan occasionally, until sugar dissolves. Increase heat and boil 1 minute. Cool 5 minutes. Combine flour and baking soda. Add to honey mixture. Blend in fruit and nut mixture. Spread batter evenly in prepared pan, using moistened spatula. Bake until cake pulls from sides of pan, about 45 minutes. Cool completely before removing from pan. Trim edges as necessary. (*Can be wrapped in foil and stored at room temperature 2 weeks.*) Before serving, arrange reserved fruit and whole almonds decoratively atop cake.

Old-Fashioned Gingerbread House

This recipe, which can be halved, makes enough dough for two houses, one to keep and one to give. Use cardboard patterns for each portion of the house, or roll the dough out and use a ruler on it to create the various shapes. These step-by-step instructions apply to making the cardboard patterns as well as tracing the measurements directly on the gingerbread dough.

Makes 2

Gingerbread
1⅓ cups honey
1 cup sugar

8 to 8½ cups all purpose flour
3 tablespoons baking soda
2 tablespoons cinnamon
4 teaspoons ground ginger
1 tablespoon ground allspice
¾ cup milk
2 eggs, room temperature

Milk
12 blanched whole almonds
1 glacéed cherry, halved

Royal Icing
2⅔ cups powdered sugar, sifted
2 egg whites, room temperature
2 tablespoons fresh lemon juice
Almond extract

Cinnamon sticks
Candies

Powdered sugar

Patterns:
For base: Cut out 10 × 10-inch square.
For roof: Cut out 5 × 7½-inch rectangle.
For house sides: Cut 4 × 4½-inch rectangle.
For house front and back: Cut out 4½ × 7-inch rectangle. To form peaked roof line, cut from center of one 4½-inch side to point 3 inches down right side,

cutting off corner. Make second cut starting at same place on 4¹/₂-inch side and cuting to point 3 inches down left side, cutting off another corner.

For chimney: Cut 1¹/₂ × 3-inch rectangle for chimney front. Cut 1¹/₂-inch square for chimney back. Cut 1¹/₄ × 3-inch rectangle for chimney sides; cut sloped edge by making diagonal cut from center of left 3-inch side to opposite corner, cutting off one corner.

For gingerbread: Heat honey and sugar in heavy small saucepan over low heat, swirling pan occasionally, until sugar dissolves. Increase heat and bring just to simmer. Cool to lukewarm.

Combine 8 cups flour, baking soda, cinnamon, ginger and allspice in heavy-duty mixer fitted with dough hook. (Can also be mixed by hand.) Add honey mixture, ³/₄ cup milk and eggs and beat just until smooth. Knead dough on lightly floured surface until no longer sticky, adding more flour if necessary. Wrap tightly and let stand 2 hours. (*Can be prepared 1 week ahead and refrigerated. Bring to room temperature before continuing.*)

Preheat oven to 375°F. Line baking sheets with parchment. Divide dough into 5 pieces. Roll out 1 piece at a time on lightly floured surface to ³/₁₆-inch-thick rectangle (keep remaining pieces tightly wrapped). Cut out gingerbread pieces, using patterns as guide. Cut out 2 base pieces. Transfer to prepared sheets. Cut out 4 roof pieces. Transfer to prepared sheets. Press shingle design into each roof piece, using round cookie cutter and making indentations parallel to longer side.

Cut out 4 house side pieces. Transfer to prepared sheets. To form windows, cut H in center of each side piece, with sides of H parallel to 4¹/₂-inch-long sides of dough; sides of H should be 2 inches long and crossbar 1 inch long. Fold windows partially open and hold in place with foil ball.

Cut 2 chimney front and 2 chimney back pieces. Cut 4 chimney sides, 2 with sloped edge facing right and 2 with sloped edge facing left. Transfer pieces to prepared sheets.

Cut out 2 house front pieces and 2 house back pieces, using same pattern. Transfer to prepared sheets. To cut out 2³/₄ × 1¹/₂-inch front door on 1 front piece: Start cutting on 4¹/₂-inch side 1 inch from one 4-inch side; make 2³/₄-inch side parallel to 4-inch side. Transfer door to clear area on prepared sheets. Repeat, cutting door in second front piece; transfer to clear area.

Gather dough scraps and reroll. Cut out snowmen, trees and snowdrifts if desired. Transfer to prepared sheets.

Brush gingerbread with milk and pierce all over with fork. Arrange almonds in flower pattern in center of peak on both house front pieces; press into dough. Press cherry half in center of almond designs. Bake gingerbread until just golden brown, about 8 minutes. Transfer to racks and cool.

For icing: Using electric mixer, beat 1¹/₃ cups sugar, 1 egg white, 1 tablespoon lemon juice and dash of almond extract just until peaks form. Keep icing covered when not working with it.

To assemble: Brush loose flour off all gingerbread pieces. Arrange 1 base on surface. Spoon icing into pastry bag fitted with medium plain tip (no. 3). Starting 1 inch from back edge of base and 3 inches in from one side, pipe ¹/₂ × 4¹/₂-inch icing line parallel to back edge. Starting at each end of line, pipe 2 more ¹/₂ × 4¹/₂-inch lines parallel to sides. Turn one back piece upper side down on work surface. Pipe ¹/₂-inch-wide icing line along inner edge of both 4-inch sides. Position back upright on icing along back of base, icing side facing inward; press to secure. Position 2 side pieces, windows opening out, on remaining icing lines on base, pressing into back and base. Pipe ¹/₂-inch-wide line on base between ends of sides, leaving space for door. Pipe icing in line along back edge of each 4-inch side of front piece. Position front on icing on base and press into base and sides. Let house stand until icing is firm, about 15 minutes.

Pipe icing along top edges of front and back pieces. Set 2 roof pieces on edges, 7¹/₂-inch sides parallel to base. Secure with toothpicks. Pipe icing along edge where 2 roof pieces meet. Let stand until firm, about 3 hours.

Gently twist toothpicks out of roof. Pipe line of icing along one edge of chimney back. Place on your left of roof when facing front of house, parallel to and 1 inch down from roof peak. Pipe icing on back side of 1¹/₂-inch side of 2 chimney side pieces, 1 with sloped edge facing right and 1 with sloped edge facing left; pipe icing along edge of sloped edges. Position on roof, one on each side of chimney back, 1¹/₂-inch sides touching edge of chimney back and slope on roof; press to secure. Pipe icing along both 3-inch edges and one 1¹/₂-inch edge of chimney front. Position on roof between chimney sides placing iced 1¹/₂-inch side down; press to secure. Pipe icing on one 1¹/₂-inch edge and one 3-inch edge of door. Position slightly ajar in door opening; press to secure. Form cinnamon sticks in stack on base to resemble wood pile; secure with icing. Pipe icing on as desired to form snow on roof, icicles hanging from eaves, outlining shutters, walks, etc. Attach cutout snowmen, trees, snowdrifts and candies with icing.

Make second batch of icing as above, using remaining 1¹/₃ cups sugar, 1 egg white, 1 tablespoon lemon juice and dash of almond extract. Assemble second house with remaining gingerbread pieces as above. Let both houses dry 12 hours. Dust lightly with powdered sugar. (*Can be wrapped in large plastic bag and stored for 3 weeks at room temperature; do not refrigerate.*)

Sweet Semolina Diamonds

Semolina flour, made from durum wheat, is the basis of many pastas. It is combined here with sugar and all purpose flour to produce a slightly sweet, crunchy rum-raisin cookie.

Makes about 3 dozen

1 cup light rum
1 cup golden raisins

4 egg yolks, room temperature
1 cup sugar

2 cups all purpose flour
1¹/₂ cups semolina flour
1 cup (2 sticks) unsalted butter, melted and cooled

1 teaspoon vanilla
   Grated peel of 1 lemon
¹/₄ teaspoon salt
¹/₂ cup pine nuts
2 tablespoons powdered sugar

Combine rum and raisins in small bowl and set aside several hours (or overnight) to plump. Drain raisins, reserving liquid. Pat raisins dry.

Preheat oven to 375°F. Generously butter baking sheets. Beat yolks and sugar in large bowl of electric mixer until slowly dissolving ribbon forms when beaters are lifted, 7 minutes.

Combine flours and gradually mix into egg mixture. Blend in melted butter, vanilla, lemon peel, salt and reserved raisin liquid. Fit mixer with dough hook or turn dough out onto lightly floured surface. Knead until smooth, about 5 minutes. Sprinkle raisins and nuts over dough and continue kneading just until incorporated. Lightly flour work surface again. Roll dough out to thickness of ¹/₃ inch. Using very sharp knife, cut dough diagonally into 2-inch-wide strips, then cut diagonally in opposite direction to form diamonds. Transfer diamonds to baking sheets, spacing evenly. Bake until cookies are lightly colored, about 20 minutes. Serve warm or at room temperature. Store in airtight container. Sprinkle with powdered sugar before serving.

Maple Syrup Shortbreads

Makes about 36

Shortbread
1/2 cup (1 stick) unsalted butter, room temperature
1/4 cup sugar
1 cup all purpose flour

Maple Topping
3/4 cup firmly packed brown sugar
1/3 cup pure maple syrup

1 tablespoon unsalted butter, room temperature
1 egg, room temperature
1 teaspoon vanilla
1/2 cup chopped toasted walnuts

For shortbread: Preheat oven to 350°F. Generously butter 9-inch square baking dish. Cream butter and sugar in processor until light and fluffy. Add flour and process just until blended; do not form ball. Pat into bottom of prepared dish. Bake until shortbread is light brown, about 25 minutes.

For topping: Beat sugar, maple syrup and butter to blend. Beat in egg and vanilla. Pour over shortbread. Sprinkle evenly with walnuts. Bake until topping is set, about 25 minutes. Cool shortbread on rack. Cut into 1 1/2-inch squares. Store in airtight container.

Mocha Chocolate Chip Cookies

Makes about 7 dozen

3 cups semisweet chocolate chips
1/2 cup (1 stick) butter
4 ounces unsweetened chocolate

1/2 cup all purpose flour
1/2 teaspoon baking powder
1/2 teaspoon salt

4 eggs, room temperature
1 1/2 cups sugar
1 1/2 tablespoons instant coffee powder
2 teaspoons vanilla

Melt 1 1/2 cups chocolate chips, butter and unsweetened chocolate in top of double boiler set over hot (but not boiling) water. Stir until smooth. Remove from over water.

Preheat oven to 350°F. Line baking sheets with parchment or waxed paper. Combine flour, baking powder and salt. Beat eggs, sugar, coffee powder and vanilla in large bowl of electric mixer at high speed 2 minutes. Stir in chocolate mixture, then flour. Add remaining 1 1/2 cups chocolate chips. Drop batter onto prepared sheets by teaspoons, spacing evenly. Bake until cookies are crackled and shiny outside but still soft inside, about 8 minutes; do not overbake. Cool completely before removing from sheets. Store in airtight container.

For variation, add 2 cups chopped toasted pecans to batter.

Windmill Cookies

Makes about 2 dozen

8 ounces cream cheese, room temperature
3/4 cup (1 1/2 sticks) unsalted butter, room temperature
1 egg yolk
1 1/2 cups all purpose flour
1 tablespoon baking powder

1/2 cup (about) strawberry jam or currant jelly

Powdered sugar

Beat cream cheese, butter and yolk in large bowl until smooth. Blend in flour and baking powder to form stiff dough. Divide in half. Wrap in plastic and flatten into disc. Refrigerate 1 hour.

Preheat oven to 350°F. Roll out half of dough between 2 sheets of plastic wrap to thickness of ⅛ inch. Cut into 3-inch squares. Transfer to ungreased baking sheets. On each square, make cut from each corner almost to center. Fold every other corner to center and press to seal. Place about 1 teaspoon jam or jelly in center of windmill. Bake until light golden, about 14 to 16 minutes. Transfer to rack. Repeat with remaining dough. Let cookies cool completely.

Sift powdered sugar lightly over cookies. Store in airtight container.

Walnut Praline Chocolate Chip Cookies

Makes about 2½ dozen

1 cup all purpose flour
½ teaspoon salt
½ teaspoon baking soda
½ cup (1 stick) unsalted butter, room temperature
¼ cup firmly packed light brown sugar
¼ cup sugar
1 egg

1¼ cups coarsely chopped walnut praline (see Praline recipe, page 111)
⅔ cup semisweet chocolate chips

Coarsely chopped walnut praline (see Praline recipe, page 111)

Preheat oven to 350°F. Butter baking sheets. Sift flour, salt and baking soda. Using electric mixer, cream butter. Add both sugars and beat until smooth. Beat in egg. Stir in flour, then 1¼ cups praline and chocolate chips.

Drop dough onto prepared sheets, using 2 teaspoons dough for each cookie and spacing 3 inches apart. Flatten each cookie slightly with back of fork dipped in water. Sprinkle center of each with pinch of praline. Bake cookies until brown, about 10 minutes. Cool on pan 3 minutes. Transfer to racks and cool completely.

Nürnberger Lebkuchen Bars with Lemon Glaze

Let these German Christmas cookies develop their true flavor by mellowing up to two weeks before serving. They are traditionally presented in colorful tins tied with ribbon and decorated with pine sprigs and miniature pine cones. Mulled wine, brandy-laced tea or hot chocolate are appropriate complements to this dessert.

Makes 25 bars

1 cup wild honey
¾ cup firmly packed light brown sugar
2 large eggs, beaten to blend
½ cup minced candied citron
2 tablespoons kirsch
1 tablespoon grated lemon peel
1 teaspoon cinnamon
1 teaspoon ground aniseed
¾ teaspoon ground allspice
¾ teaspoon freshly grated nutmeg
¾ teaspoon salt
½ teaspoon ground cloves
½ cup lukewarm strained tea

⅓ cup (generous) finely chopped toasted almonds
⅓ cup (generous) finely chopped toasted husked hazelnuts

2½ cups unbleached all purpose flour
1 cup finely ground almonds
1 cup finely ground hazelnuts
1 teaspoon baking soda
1 teaspoon baking powder

Lemon Sugar Glaze*
25 candied red cherry halves
100 whole blanched almonds

Heat honey in heavy small saucepan over low heat until bubbly and slightly darkened. Remove from heat. Add brown sugar and stir to dissolve. Turn into large bowl. Cool.

Whisk eggs into honey mixture. Mix in next 9 ingredients. Stir in tea and chopped almonds and hazelnuts.

Sift together flour, ground nuts, baking soda and baking powder. Repeat. Using electric mixer, gradually beat dry ingredients into honey mixture; dough will be very soft and sticky. Cover with plastic wrap, then towel. Refrigerate overnight or up to 2 days. Let stand at room temperature 30 minutes before proceeding with recipe.

Preheat oven to 375°F. Line bottom and sides of baking sheet with parchment. Transfer dough to prepared sheet, spreading evenly to ½ inch thickness. Bake until golden brown, 15 to 20 minutes. Cool slightly in pan.

Using parchment as aid, slide lebkuchen onto work surface. Cut lengthwise into five 2-inch rows. Cut crosswise into five 3-inch rows for total of 25 bars. Using spatula and working quickly, spread glaze in thin film over top of each bar. Set cherry half in center of each. Arrange 4 almonds around each cherry to form flower. Layer bars in airtight container between sheets of waxed paper. Store at room temperature.

*Lemon Sugar Glaze

Makes about 1 cup

1⅓ cups powdered sugar	2 tablespoons kirsch
6 tablespoons cornstarch	Hot water
2 tablespoons fresh lemon juice, strained	

Sift sugar and cornstarch into bowl. Whisk in lemon juice and kirsch. Whisk in enough hot water 1 tablespoon at a time to form thick, smooth paste.

Toffee Fudge Brownies

These are dark, moist and crunchy, with bits of chocolate toffee candy.

Makes twenty-five 1¾-inch squares

6 chocolate-covered toffee bars (6⅜ ounces total), broken into small pieces	½ cup (1 stick) unsalted butter, cut into 4 pieces, room temperature
1 cup walnut pieces	4 eggs
1¼ cups sugar	1 tablespoon vanilla
5 ounces unsweetened chocolate, broken into pieces	¼ teaspoon salt
	⅔ cup unbleached all purpose flour

Position rack in center of oven and preheat to 325°F. Grease and flour 9-inch square baking pan.

Combine toffee and walnuts in processor and chop coarsely using 6 to 8 on/off turns. Remove from work bowl and set aside. Combine sugar and chocolate in work bowl and mix using 6 on/off turns, then process until chocolate is as fine as sugar, about 1 minute. Add butter and blend 1 minute. Add eggs, vanilla and salt and blend until fluffy, about 40 seconds, stopping as necessary to scrape down sides of work bowl. Add flour and toffee mixture and blend using 4 to 5 on/off turns, just until flour is incorporated; do not overprocess (remove blade and blend mixture gently with spatula if necessary to mix in flour completely). Turn batter into prepared pan, spreading evenly. Bake until tester inserted in center comes out almost clean, about 50 minutes (for firmer, cakelike brownies, bake about 5 minutes longer). Let cool in pan on rack. Cut into 1¾-inch squares. Store in airtight container.

Brown Sugar Pecan Brownies

Makes about 3 dozen

2½ cups all purpose flour
1 pound light brown sugar
1 cup (2 sticks) unsalted butter, cut into ½-inch pieces

2 eggs, room temperature
1 teaspoon vanilla

1½ teaspoons baking powder
   Pinch of salt
1 cup pecans, chopped

Preheat oven to 350°F. Lightly butter 9 × 13-inch baking pan. Combine 1¼ cups flour with ⅓ cup brown sugar in medium bowl. Cut in ½ cup butter until mixture resembles coarse meal. Press into bottom of prepared pan. Bake 15 minutes (retain oven at 350°F).

Meanwhile, cook remaining brown sugar and ½ cup butter in medium saucepan over low heat until sugar dissolves. Beat eggs in large bowl of electric mixer until pale yellow and ribbon forms when beaters are lifted. Gradually beat in brown sugar mixture. Stir in vanilla, blending thoroughly.

Sift remaining 1¼ cups flour with baking powder and salt. Blend into brown sugar mixture. Stir in pecans. Spread mixture over baked crust. Bake 25 minutes. Cool in pan on rack. Cut into squares. Wrap brownies tightly in plastic and store in airtight container.

Rococo's Brownies

The ultimate brownies: moist, dense, studded with walnuts and topped with an old-fashioned frosting.

Makes 8

Brownies
⅔ cup all purpose flour
7 tablespoons unsweetened cocoa powder
½ teaspoon baking powder
½ teaspoon salt
10½ tablespoons butter
1 cup sugar
1 teaspoon vanilla
2 eggs, room temperature
2 tablespoons dark corn syrup
1 cup coarsely chopped walnuts

Frosting
2¼ ounces unsweetened chocolate
3 tablespoons butter
1½ cups powdered sugar
3 tablespoons hot water
¾ teaspoon vanilla

⅓ cup coarsely chopped walnuts

For brownies: Preheat oven to 350°F. Line 8-inch square baking pan with parchment paper; butter and flour paper. Sift together flour, cocoa powder, baking powder and salt. Repeat twice. Set aside. Using electric mixer, cream butter with sugar and vanilla until light and fluffy. Beat in eggs 1 at a time. Blend in corn syrup. Mix in dry ingredients. Stir in walnuts. Pour batter into prepared pan, spreading evenly. Bake until tester inserted in center comes out clean, about 30 minutes. Cool. Remove from pan.

For frosting: Melt chocolate and butter in double boiler over simmering water. Stir until smooth. Mix in sugar, water and vanilla.

Spread frosting over brownie. Sprinkle with walnuts. Let stand until frosting is set. Cut brownie into squares to serve.

7 ❦ Candy

Most of us never outgrow our love for candy, and a gift of a homemade sweet is extra special, extra rich and extra good. And candy is surprisingly easy to make: Once you learn the basics (be sure to have an accurate candy thermometer, and see the box on page 109 for chocolate tempering techniques), you'll discover a whole world of cooking pleasure.

This chapter has something for everyone and for every season. Try anything from simple treats like Fruit and Nut Rolls (page 100) and Rocky Road (page 103)—easy enough for a child to make—to impressive confections such as Grand Marnier Chocolate Truffles (page 108) and Peanut Butter Feuilleté (page 106) served in a Nougat Candy Dish (page 104). Chocolate-Covered Brandied Cherries (page 112) and Marzipan Fruit and Animals (page 114) are favorites with both young and old.

Appropriate gift packaging for candies can run the gamut from the traditional, such as covered glass jars and foil-lined boxes, to the frivolous, such as simple tin buckets decorated with silver stars and streamers, a miniature jewelry box or a toy truck. Whether the look is romantic, festive or just plain fun, candy is the ultimate gift.

Caramelized Orange Sections

Dry the orange sections several hours ahead and let stand at room temperature. These are best served the same day you prepare them.

Makes about 30

1 **pound sugar**
Fresh lemon juice (optional)

3 **oranges, peeled and divided into segments (skins intact)**

Line baking sheet with waxed paper. Melt sugar in heavy 5-inch-wide saucepan over high heat, stirring constantly with wooden spoon so sugar melts evenly and develops golden caramel color. Remove from heat. (If caramelized sugar is too dark, lighten with 2 to 3 drops fresh lemon juice.) Dry orange segments with paper towels. Dip one end of each segment into caramel. Place on baking sheet. Let cool until set. Dip other end of oranges in caramel so entire segment is covered (if caramel solidifies, reheat over gently simmering water until liquefied).

If larger saucepan is used, more sugar syrup may be needed to coat sections.

Fruit and Nut Rolls

A processor makes this easy. Most machines will be able to handle this recipe in four batches.

Makes 3¹/₂ pounds (10 1 × 10-inch rolls or about 142 ¹/₂-inch slices)

1 **pound dried figs**
12 **ounces pitted dates**
8 **ounces dried apricots**
³/₄ **pound walnut pieces (3 cups)**
8 **ounces currants (2 cups)**
¹/₂ **cup sugar**

¹/₂ **cup honey cream or spun honey**
1¹/₂ **cups shredded coconut**

Combine figs, dates and apricots in plastic bag and place in freezer for 10 minutes. Combine walnuts, currants and sugar in small bowl and mix well.

Set large bowl near processor. Insert steel knife in processor and add about ¹/₄ of fig and walnut mixtures. Chop using on/off turns until finely minced. Transfer to large bowl. Repeat 3 times.

Using hands, work in honey with kneading motion. Divide mixture into 5 parts and roll each into cylinder 1 inch in diameter. Cut each in half. Roll in coconut and cut into slices about ¹/₂ inch thick. Wrap in waxed paper and store in airtight can in refrigerator.

Caramel Moux

Soft and smooth in the French style.

Makes about forty 1-inch squares

3 **cups sugar**
2 **cups whipping cream**

¹/₂ **cup light corn syrup**
1 **1-inch piece vanilla bean**

Butter 9-inch square or springform pan. Combine all ingredients in heavy 4-quart saucepan (mixture should not fill more than ¹/₃ of pan). Cook over medium-high heat until candy thermometer registers 250°F (hard-ball stage), shaking pan gently to dissolve sugar and stirring as little as possible with wooden spoon. Pour into prepared pan (*to avoid crystallization, do not scrape out saucepan*). Cool until just firm but not hard. Cut into 1-inch squares. Wrap in plastic or waxed paper. Store in foil-lined airtight container up to 6 weeks.

Creamy Caramels

These are nothing like the kind you buy at the store.

Makes about 7 dozen 1-inch squares

1½ cups half and half
1½ cups whipping cream
2 cups sugar
¼ teaspoon salt
1⅓ cups light corn syrup

2 teaspoons vanilla
1 cup chopped toasted walnuts (optional)

Butter 9-inch square pan. Combine half and half and cream in 4-cup measure. Mix sugar, salt, corn syrup and 1 cup of the combined creams in heavy 3- or 4-quart saucepan. Cook over medium-high heat, stirring constantly, until syrup reaches 234°F on candy thermometer (soft-ball stage).

Add 1 more cup of cream and stir until mixture again reaches 234°F. Add remaining cream and stir until mixture reaches 250°F (hard-ball stage); *this could take up to 1 hour.* Remove from heat and stir in vanilla and nuts. Pour into pan and refrigerate until just firm but not hard. Cut in pieces about 1 inch square and wrap in cellophane, plastic wrap or waxed paper.

Nutmegs

Makes about 12 dozen

¼ cup (½ stick) butter
1 cup whipping cream
2 pounds milk chocolate, grated
1 teaspoon freshly grated nutmeg

Powdered sugar

12 ounces semisweet chocolate, grated and tempered (see box, page 109)

Melt butter in cream in heavy large saucepan over medium heat, then bring to boil. Remove from heat. Stir in 2 pounds grated chocolate with wooden spoon until melted and smooth. Mix in nutmeg. Cool chocolate mixture in saucepan several hours or overnight.

Line baking sheet with waxed paper. Warm pan quickly over low heat, then invert to release chocolate in one piece. Cut into ½-inch slices, then into cubes. Dust cubes lightly with powdered sugar, shaking off excess. Roll cubes between palms into nutmeg-size balls. Set on baking sheet.

Line another baking sheet with waxed paper. Pour powdered sugar into shallow pan. Dip each candy into tempered chocolate with candy spoon or dipping fork, covering completely, then roll in powdered sugar. Arrange on prepared baking sheet. Make slight indentation with fork tines to resemble nutmeg nuts. Store in foil-lined airtight container in cool dry place up to 6 weeks.

If candy spoon or dipping fork is unavailable, use fondue fork or tip of small sharp knife.

Chocolate Cutouts

Serve these pretty candies with cookies and ice cream for dessert.

Makes about 40

8 ounces semisweet chocolate, coarsely chopped

Powdered sugar or unsweetened cocoa powder

Line baking sheet with waxed paper. Melt chocolate in double boiler over barely simmering water. Whisk until smooth. Spread 1/8 inch thick on prepared sheet. Refrigerate until firm but not brittle, about 2 hours.

Soften chocolate 5 minutes at room temperature. Cut into desired shapes using hors d'oeuvre cutters. Store in airtight container in freezer. Dust with sugar or cocoa before serving.

Deluxe Holiday Mints

Makes about 70 pieces

1 pound sugar
1/2 cup water
1/4 cup light corn syrup

1 teaspoon mint extract
1 to 2 drops green food coloring

Dampen marble or other nonwooden work surface. Prepare 1/16-inch paper cone or fit pastry bag with No. 2 tip. Line baking sheet with waxed paper.

Stir sugar, water and corn syrup in heavy medium saucepan with wooden spoon until sugar dissolves. Bring to boil without stirring over medium-high heat, washing down crystals on sides of pan with wet pastry brush. Boil until candy thermometer registers 234°F (soft-ball stage).

Pour mixture onto dampened surface. Working with dough scraper or spatula, lift and fold mixture repeatedly from edges to center until silky and pure white. Fondant will stiffen to where it no longer can be kneaded.

Turn mixture into heavy large saucepan and warm very carefully over low heat to 105°F to 110°F, stirring constantly; do not overheat or fondant will become runny and lose shine. Remove from heat and stir in mint extract and green food coloring.

Pour fondant into prepared paper cone or pastry bag and pipe small circles onto prepared sheet. Let cool until firm. Store mints in foil- or waxed paper-lined airtight container in cool dry place for up to 6 weeks.

Almond-Walnut Butter Toffee

Makes about 2 pounds

2 1/4 cups sugar
1 1/4 cups (2 1/2 sticks) butter
1/2 cup water
1 teaspoon salt
1 1/2 cups chopped blanched almonds (about 8 ounces)

1 cup chopped walnuts (about 6 ounces)
6 ounces semisweet or milk chocolate, melted

Generously butter 9 × 13-inch baking dish and set aside. Combine sugar, butter, water and salt in 3-quart saucepan and bring to boil over medium-high heat. Continue cooking, stirring constantly with wooden spoon, until mixture registers 325°F on candy thermometer. Stir in almonds and 1/2 cup walnuts. Pour into prepared pan, spreading evenly. Let cool. Spread with melted chocolate and sprinkle with remaining walnuts. Break toffee into pieces before serving.

Bittersweet Chocolate Caramels with Burnt Almonds

While best enjoyed within ten days of preparation, these heirloom candies will keep up to one month. Pack them—and the recipe—into an apothecary jar or other attractive container.

Makes 6 to 7 dozen

1¹/₂ cups sugar
³/₄ cup light corn syrup
¹/₄ cup (¹/₂ stick) unsalted butter, cut into small pieces
2 tablespoons cold water
1 tablespoon amaretto liqueur
3 ounces unsweetened chocolate, melted

1 cup whipping cream, scalded and hot
10 ounces whole unblanched almonds, chopped into 2 to 3 pieces each, toasted
2 teaspoons vanilla
¹/₄ teaspoon (generous) salt

Lightly butter 11 × 15-inch nonstick baking sheet. Cook sugar, corn syrup, butter, water and liqueur in heavy, deep, narrow saucepan over low heat until sugar dissolves, swirling pan occasionally. Bring to boil. Reduce heat to medium-low. Stir in melted chocolate and simmer gently until candy thermometer registers 234°F to 240°F (soft-ball stage). Gradually stir in cream (be careful; mixture may spatter) and cook, stirring constantly, until candy thermometer registers 244°F to 248°F (firm-ball stage). Remove from heat. Stir in almonds, vanilla and salt. Pour caramel onto prepared sheet, tilting sheet to cover completely. Let caramel cool about 15 minutes.

Using heavy chef's knife, cut caramel lengthwise into six 1³/₄-inch-wide strips. Peel off each strip. Using hands, form and squeeze each strip into 24-inch roll. Cut each roll crosswise into 1³/₄-inch pieces. Wrap each piece in 4¹/₂ ×6-inch piece of plastic wrap or waxed paper. Roll up tightly, then twist ends. Store in airtight container.

Chocolate Peanut Clusters

Makes about 2¹/₂ dozen 1¹/₂-inch clusters

4 ounces semisweet chocolate
4 ounces milk chocolate
1 teaspoon oil

2 cups cocktail peanuts (remove some of salt by shaking nuts in strainer)

Line large baking sheet with waxed paper. Combine chocolate and oil in top of double boiler and melt over hot, not boiling, water. *Do not allow any water to drop into chocolate; this would cause it to thicken.* Stir until blended. Add peanuts and mix until coated.

Drop by scant tablespoons onto waxed paper. Chill in refrigerator until firm. Serve directly from refrigerator.

Rocky Road

Makes 3 dozen 1¹/₂-inch squares

8 ounces milk chocolate
8 ounces semisweet chocolate
1 tablespoon unsalted butter
Pinch of salt
1 teaspoon vanilla

20 marshmallows, snipped into quarters
³/₄ cups coarsely chopped toasted walnuts

Butter 8-inch square pan. Melt chocolate with butter and salt in top of double boiler over very hot, not boiling water. Add vanilla, marshmallows and nuts and stir thoroughly. Spread in pan and chill until firm. Cut into squares. (*If candy is difficult to cut, let stand at room temperature about 10 minutes.*)

Nougat Candy Dish

A pretty display for other homemade candies—and just as delicious. Use the remaining trimmings for the filling of the Coconut Snowballs (see recipe, page 108)

Makes 1

Vegetable oil

2 cups sugar

1¹/₃ cups sliced blanched almonds

2 ounces semisweet chocolate

1 teaspoon water or kirsch

Generously oil marble or other nonwooden work surface, rolling pin and outside of inverted medium-size stainless steel mixing bowl.

Melt sugar in heavy small skillet over high heat, stirring constantly with wooden spoon so sugar melts evenly to golden caramel color. Reduce heat to low and stir until all sugar lumps dissolve. Stir in almonds. Pour onto oiled surface. Working quickly, roll nougat with oiled rolling pin to ³/₁₆- to ¹/₄-inch thickness. Cut out 9-inch circle with sharp knife. Place immediately (while still warm and pliable) on outside of inverted oiled bowl, pressing evenly and arranging on bowl as far down sides as possible. Cool nougat completely on mixing bowl.

Cut three ³/₄ × 3-inch strips from nougat trimmings (if necessary, rewarm trimmings over low heat to make pliable). Overlap short ends to create slightly flattened loops; these will be "feet" for dish. Carefully loosen cooled nougat from bowl. Set open side up.

Melt chocolate in top of double boiler over gently simmering water. Stir in water or kirsch. Transfer mixture to pastry bag fitted with star tip. Invert bowl onto work surface. Pipe small amount of chocolate to secure "feet" to bottom of bowl. Let chocolate cool until set. Turn bowl over and pipe chocolate border around edge. Let cool completely before using dish.

Almond Bark

Make this quick treat in the microwave.

Makes about 1¹/₂ pounds

1 cup blanched whole almonds

1 teaspoon butter

1 pound white chocolate, broken into pieces

Combine almonds and butter in 9-inch glass pie plate and cook in microwave on High, stirring once or twice, until almonds are toasted, about 4 to 5 minutes.

Line baking sheet with waxed paper and set aside. Cook chocolate in 2-quart bowl on High just until softened, about 1¹/₂ to 2 minutes; *do not overcook or chocolate will become grainy*. Stir in almonds and blend well. Spread mixture onto baking sheet. Refrigerate until set. Break into pieces to serve.

Nougat Montelimar

Cooking the sugar in a small, narrow, deep pan lets it cook to the hard-crack stage without turning brown.

Makes about seventy-two 1¹/₂ × ³/₄-inch pieces

2 cups sugar

¹/₂ cup water

¹/₂ cup honey

2 egg whites

3 ounces white chocolate, melted

1 cup blanched almonds, toasted

1 cup filberts (hazelnuts), toasted and husked

¹/₂ cup pistachios, blanched, husked and dried

¹/₂ cup quartered candied cherries

2 phyllo pastry sheets

Stir sugar and water in heavy, narrow, deep saucepan with wooden spoon until sugar dissolves. Bring to boil without stirring over high heat, washing down crystals on sides of pan with wet pastry brush. Boil until candy thermometer registers 305°F (hard-crack stage).

Meanwhile, heat honey and egg whites in top of double boiler over gently simmering water to 120°F. Transfer to large bowl of electric mixer and beat until stiff peaks form.

With mixer running at low speed, gradually pour hot syrup into egg white mixture. Stir in melted white chocolate with wooden spoon. Fold in nuts and candied cherries.

Place 1 phyllo pastry sheet on parchment paper on work surface. Spread nougat mixture over. Cover with remaining sheet of phyllo. Roll to 3/4- to 1-inch thickness. Let cool.

Cut candy crosswise into 1 1/2-inch strips. Cut strips into 3/4-inch pieces or diamond shapes. Brush off as much phyllo as possible. Wrap candy in plastic or waxed paper. Store nougat in foil- or waxed paper-lined airtight container in cool dry place up to 6 weeks.

Gianduja "Bacon"

A combination of praline and chocolate is layered to resemble bacon for this unusual confection.

Makes about 14 dozen 1/2-inch pieces

Praline Paste
1 pound filberts (hazelnuts), toasted and husked
8 ounces (2 cups plus 2 tablespoons) powdered sugar
2 tablespoons corn oil

Chocolate Layers
1 pound semisweet chocolate
1 pound milk chocolate

3 tablespoons kirsch
2 tablespoons Grand Marnier

1 pound semisweet chocolate, grated and tempered (see box, page 109)

For praline paste: Puree all ingredients in processor using on/off turns until mixture is oily paste resembling peanut butter, scraping bowl frequently.

For layers: Melt semisweet and milk chocolate separately in top of double boiler over gently simmering water to 110°F. Transfer to separate bowls. Do not let chocolate cool. Beat 3/4 pound (1 1/2 cups) praline paste into each. Add kirsch to semisweet chocolate and Grand Marnier to milk chocolate. Divide each mixture in half. Roll half at a time between 2 sheets of plastic wrap into 12 × 15-inch rectangle. To ensure even sheet, flip over and roll other side. Repeat with remaining halves. Cool rectangles 1 hour at room temperature or refrigerate 10 minutes to facilitate removing plastic. When cooled, stack 4 rectangles on baking sheet, alternating semisweet and milk chocolate. Trim edges. Cut rectangles lengthwise into 1 1/2-inch strips.

Line baking sheet with waxed paper. Brush strips on all sides with tempered chocolate, brushing in one direction only. Let stand on prepared sheet until set. Cut crosswise into 1/2-inch strips. Store in foil-lined airtight container in cool dry place up to 6 weeks.

English Butter Toffee

Makes 1 pound 6 ounces

1 cup sugar
1 cup (2 sticks) unsalted butter
1/4 cup water
1/2 teaspoon salt
1 teaspoon vanilla

4 ounces milk chocolate
4 ounces sweet cooking chocolate (best quality)
1/4 cup finely chopped toasted pecans or walnuts

Butter 10 × 15-inch baking sheet. Combine sugar, butter, water and salt in heavy saucepan. Place over medium-high heat and bring to boil, stirring until sugar is dissolved. Continue boiling, shaking pan occasionally, until candy thermometer registers 305°F (hard-crack stage). Remove from heat and stir in vanilla. Pour onto baking sheet in 10 × 10-inch square. Let stand until cool and hardened.

Melt 2 ounces of each chocolate in small pan over very low heat. Spread evenly with spatula on top side of toffee. Immediately sprinkle with half of nuts. Refrigerate for 30 minutes.

Using spatula, carefully turn toffee over. Repeat with remaining chocolate and nuts. Return to refrigerator and chill for at least 30 minutes.

When firm enough to handle, break toffee into pieces. Store in airtight container in cool, dry place.

Instead of combining milk chocolate and sweet cooking chocolate, toffee can be coated with 8 ounces of either type.

Peanut Butter Feuilleté

Makes about 48

1 pound sugar
¼ cup (½ stick) unsalted butter
¾ cup unsalted natural peanut butter

12 ounces semisweet chocolate, grated and tempered (see box, page 109)

Preheat oven to 300°F. Oil marble or other nonwooden work surface. Oil heavy baking sheet. Melt sugar in heavy large saucepan over medium heat until caramel colored, stirring constantly with wooden spoon. Stir in butter until melted. Pour mixture onto prepared surface and spread into 12 × 12-inch square using metal spatula. Working quickly, spread peanut butter over ⅔ of sugar mixture. Fold plain ⅓ over center and remaining ⅓ over top as for business letter; sugar will begin to harden at this point. Immediately transfer to prepared baking sheet and heat in oven until pliable, about 4 minutes. (Any peanut butter that exudes may be placed on top.)

Rotate package 90 degrees. Roll out with oiled rolling pin on baking sheet and fold again into thirds. Rotate package 90 degrees. If sugar is still soft, roll and fold again (otherwise return to oven and reheat until pliable). After third fold, return to oven and reheat until pliable. Rotate package 90 degrees. Roll out with oiled rolling pin on baking sheet to thickness of ¼ inch. Slice into 1-inch squares. Cool.

Line baking sheet with waxed paper. Dip opposite corners of each square in tempered chocolate (or cover entire square if desired). Arrange on prepared baking sheet. Cool until set. Store feuilleté in foil-lined airtight container in cool dry place up to 6 weeks.

Chocolate Peanut Butter Balls

These candies freeze well.

Makes about 3½ dozen

1 cup chopped dates
1 cup chopped walnuts
1 cup powdered sugar, sifted
1 cup chunky peanut butter

2 tablespoons (¼ stick) butter, melted
12 squares semisweet chocolate

Line baking sheets with waxed paper. Combine dates and walnuts in large bowl. Add powdered sugar. Blend in peanut butter and melted butter and mix thoroughly. Shape into 1- to 1½-inch balls. Melt chocolate in top of double boiler set over hot (not boiling) water, stirring occasionally to prevent lumping. Dip balls into chocolate with fork, turning to coat evenly. Transfer to baking sheets. Refrigerate until chocolate is set, about 1 hour. If desired, trim bottoms of candies with knife and place in miniature muffin cup liners. Refrigerate candies until ready to serve.

Date and Peanut Butter Balls

Makes about 6 dozen
1-inch balls

1¹/₂ cups chopped walnuts or pecans
 1 cup coarsely chopped dates
 1 cup crunchy-style peanut butter
 ¹/₄ cup sifted powdered sugar
 2 tablespoons fresh lemon juice
 1 teaspoon finely grated lemon peel
 2 tablespoons (¹/₄ stick) unsalted
  butter, room temperature
 1 teaspoon vanilla
 ¹/₂ teaspoon cinnamon

Dipping Chocolate
 4 ounces milk chocolate
 4 ounces semisweet chocolate
 4 teaspoons vegetable oil

Line baking sheet with waxed paper. Combine first 9 ingredients in large bowl and mix well with wooden spoon. Chill 1 hour. Form into balls about 1 inch in diameter and place on baking sheet. Refrigerate 2 hours.

For dipping: Melt chocolate and oil in top of double boiler over hot, not boiling, water. *Do not allow any water to drop into chocolate; this would cause it to thicken.* Keep chocolate between 100°F and 110°F on candy thermometer.

Working in cool place (68°F or less), use a toothpick and teaspoon and dip balls one at a time into chocolate (tilt pan to get as much depth as possible). Return to baking sheet and refrigerate until firm. Serve chilled.

Dipping chocolate can be made with all milk chocolate or all sweet cooking chocolate if desired, using a total of 8 ounces.

Chocolate Confection with Raspberries

A terrific hostess gift.

10 to 12 servings

13 ounces semisweet chocolate
 4 lemon or other waxy leaves with
  stems, washed and dried
 4 cups fresh raspberries

Tiny strawberry leaves with buds
(optional garnish)

Melt chocolate in top of double boiler set over gently simmering water, stirring until smooth. Spread some of chocolate on underside of leaves with small spatula (do not let chocolate drip onto top of leaves). Freeze until chocolate is firm, about 10 minutes. Dip hands in ice water and dry. Remove leaf from chocolate by pulling gently from stem. Make 4 perfect leaves; return to freezer.

Line baking sheet with waxed paper. Set 14-inch rectangular flan mold on top. Remelt chocolate if necessary. Reserve 1 teaspoon melted chocolate. Spread remainder evenly inside bottom of mold (do not spread sides). Arrange berries decoratively atop chocolate; do not press down or chocolate may crack. Refrigerate only until chocolate begins to set, about 12 minutes.

Run thin-bladed knife around bottom inside edge of mold and remove. Refrigerate chocolate until completely firm. Carefully tip chocolate and remove paper. Set chocolate on serving platter. Using reserved 1 teaspoon melted chocolate (remelted if necessary), attach chocolate leaves decoratively. Refrigerate. Let stand at room temperature 30 minutes before serving. Garnish confection with tiny strawberry leaves if desired.

Roasted or caramelized whole almonds can be substituted for raspberries.

Coconut Snowballs

Delectable white chocolate truffles with coconut and crunchy nougat.

Makes 6 dozen

1 cup nougat trimmings* (see recipe for Nougat Candy Dish, page 104)
³/₄ pound imported white chocolate
2 cups flaked coconut

8 ounces imported white chocolate, tempered (see box, page 109)

Place nougat trimmings in heavy plastic bag and crush coarsely with rolling pin. Melt ³/₄ pound white chocolate in top of double boiler over gently simmering water. Add nougat and coconut and let set slightly. Roll walnut-size pieces into balls. Cool completely.

Line baking sheet with waxed paper. Dip each candy into ¹/₂ pound tempered chocolate with candy spoon or dipping fork, coating completely. Arrange on prepared sheet. Let dry completely and dip again. Store in foil- or waxed paper-lined airtight container in cool dry place up to 6 weeks.

If candy spoon or dipping fork is unavailable, use fondue fork or tip of small sharp knife.

*If not preparing Nougat Candy Dish, make small batch of nougat using ²/₃ cup sugar and scant ¹/₂ cups sliced blanched almonds. Follow instructions with dish recipe, pouring nougat out onto well-oiled nonwooden surface. Let cool completely. Break nougat into pieces, place in plastic bag and proceed with above method.

Grand Marnier Chocolate Truffles

Makes about sixty 1-inch truffles

Truffles
4 ounces sweet chocolate, broken into pieces
4 ounces milk chocolate, broken into pieces
¹/₂ teaspoon chopped orange peel (colored part only)
Pinch of salt
¹/₂ cup whipping cream, heated to simmer
1 tablespoon Grand Marnier

Dipping Chocolate
6 ounces sweet chocolate
1 tablespoon vegetable oil

2 tablespoons unsweetened cocoa powder, sifted

Line baking sheet with heavy-duty foil and grease lightly. Set aside.

Combine chocolates, orange peel and salt in processor work bowl and chop using 6 on/off turns, then process until mixture is minced, about 30 seconds. With machine running, pour hot cream through feed tube and blend until chocolate is melted. Run spatula around inside of work bowl to loosen mixture. Add Grand Marnier and blend 5 seconds. Pour onto prepared baking sheet. Refrigerate until mixture is cool and chocolate begins to firm, about 30 minutes. Return to work bowl and process until light and fluffy, about 20 seconds, stopping once to scrape down sides of bowl.

Spoon mixture into pastry bag fitted with plain ¼-inch tip. Return to refrigerator until chocolate is thick enough to be piped but is not hard, about 15 minutes. Line baking sheet with heavy-duty foil and grease lightly. Pipe mixture onto sheet in ¾-to 1-inch mounds. (Truffles can also be shaped with demitasse spoons and gently rounded with fingers.) Freeze truffles until completely firm.

For dipping chocolate: Melt chocolate with oil in top of double boiler over hot but not boiling water. Maintain chocolate between 100°F and 110°F.

Line another baking sheet with waxed paper. Working in cool area (preferably 68°F or under), dip frozen truffles into chocolate one at a time, coating completely. Arrange on prepared baking sheet. Return to freezer until firm.

Place cocoa in plastic bag. Add truffles to bag in batches of 20 and shake to coat completely. Rearrange on baking sheet and freeze. When truffles are completely frozen, transfer to plastic bags; seal airtight. Store in freezer.

Chocolate Cranberry Truffles

Makes about 4 dozen

⅔ cup fresh whole cranberries, washed

½ cup sugar

¼ cup water

2 tablespoons water

8 ounces semisweet or bittersweet chocolate

6 tablespoons (¾ stick) unsalted butter

2 tablespoons cranberry liqueur or kirsch

½ to ¾ cup unsweetened cocoa powder

Prick cranberries all over with fork. Combine ½ cup sugar and ¼ cup water in medium saucepan over low heat and cook until sugar dissolves, shaking pan occasionally. Increase heat and cook until candy thermometer registers 238°F (soft-ball stage). Add cranberries and stir until mixture is thick and

---

❧ *Chocolate Tempering Tips*

For chocolate to coat candy and fruit smoothly and with an even gloss, it must first be tempered. This involves three distinct stages.

- *Warm chocolate to 105°F to 110°F* (slightly warm to the touch). The cocoa butter in the chocolate must be completely melted before it will separate from the chocolate mass. If it is not separated, it will not emulsify back in evenly when the chocolate is later cooled, causing white streaks to form when the chocolate has firmed and set.

- *Cool chocolate to about 75°F.* Add grated chocolate to bring down the temperature. This is necessary to emulsify the mixture, or to blend the cocoa butter thoroughly back into the chocolate liquor.

- *Reheat chocolate to 91°F to 93°F.* This is the proper temperature for coating or dipping—the chocolate is now tempered. At this temperature, the cocoa butter is still emulsified, while the chocolate is warm enough to coat smoothly. If it is too cold, the coating will be too thick, and it will appear dull rather than shiny.

sticky and thermometer reaches 250°F (hard-ball stage). Let cool 1 hour, stirring occasionally.

Remove cranberries from syrup with knife and set aside. Add 2 tablespoons water to syrup. Place over low heat and simmer until syrup thickens, swirling pan occasionally. Set aside.

Melt chocolate and butter in top of double boiler set over simmering water. Stir until blended. Strain mixture through fine sieve into large bowl. Mix in cranberries, cranberry liqueur or kirsch and 2 teaspoons of cranberry syrup. Refrigerate until firm, 4 hours.

Scoop out bite-size balls from mixture using small melon baller. Pour 1/2 cup cocoa powder into flat dish. Roll truffles in cocoa until well coated, adding more cocoa powder as necessary. Transfer to paper candy cups. Arrange in container with tight-fitting lid and refrigerate. Let truffles stand at room temperature 15 minutes before serving.

Mint Truffles

A mouth-watering version of the French chocolate truffle. Undipped, they are as easy as any candy could possibly be; dipped, they are a remarkable taste experience.

Makes about 60 half-inch truffles

Chocolate
1/2 cup whipping cream
4 ounces dark sweet cooking chocolate (best quality), finely ground
4 ounces milk chocolate, finely ground
1 teaspoon peppermint extract
Pinch of salt

Dipping Chocolate (optional)
4 ounces sweet cooking chocolate
2 teaspoons vegetable oil
2 tablespoons cocoa, sifted

Line baking sheet with heavy-duty foil.

For chocolate: Heat cream in heavy 1-quart saucepan. When it begins to boil, remove from heat and add chocolate. Cover and let stand 6 minutes. Mix thoroughly with wooden spoon until chocolate is completely melted. Add peppermint and salt and pour onto foil. Refrigerate until cool and chocolate starts to firm, about 30 minutes.

Turn chocolate into processor fitted with steel knife, or into small bowl of mixer, and beat until light and fluffy.

Spoon into pastry bag fitted with plain 1/4-inch tube. Return to refrigerator until chocolate has enough body to be piped (*watch so it does not become too firm*). Grease baking sheet and pipe chocolate out in 1/2-inch diameter mounds. Place in freezer.

For dipping: Melt half of chocolate and 1 teaspoon oil in double boiler over hot, not boiling water. *Do not allow any water to drop into chocolate; this would cause it to thicken.* Keep temperature of chocolate between 100°F and 110°F on candy thermometer.

Line baking sheet with waxed paper. Working in cool place (68°F or less), dip frozen truffles one at a time into chocolate (tilt pan to get as much depth as possible). Set on baking sheet. Prepare remaining chocolate when necessary. Return truffles to freezer.

For dusting: When completely frozen, place about 20 truffles at a time into plastic bag with cocoa and shake to coat well. Return to baking sheet and freeze. When solidly frozen, transfer to airtight plastic bags. Keep in freezer.

Sunflower Seed Brittle

Makes ³/₄ pound

1 tablespoon unsalted butter
1 cup salted, dry-roasted sunflower
   seeds
¹/₄ teaspoon salt

1 cup sugar

Butter large baking sheet; set aside. Melt butter in small saucepan. Add seeds and salt and mix well. Keep warm.

    Melt sugar in heavy skillet over medium heat, stirring constantly. When sugar is golden brown, quickly stir in warm seeds. Pour out onto baking sheet and spread with wooden spoon or spatula into 10-inch square. Let cool until firm. Break into pieces and store in airtight container in cool, dry place.

Old-Fashioned Peanut Brittle

Makes 2¹/₂ pounds

2 cups sugar
1 cup light corn syrup
¹/₂ cup water
1 cup (2 sticks) unsalted butter

2¹/₂ cups dry-roasted peanuts,
   warmed
1 teaspoon baking soda
1 teaspoon vanilla

Combine sugar, corn syrup and water in heavy 3-quart saucepan. Place over medium heat and stir until sugar dissolves. When syrup comes to boil, blend in butter and stir frequently. Continue cooking until candy thermometer registers 280°F (soft-crack stage). Immediately add peanuts and stir constantly until thermometer reaches 305°F (hard-crack stage). Remove from heat and quickly add baking soda and vanilla, mixing well. Immediately pour into 2 jelly roll pans and spread as close to edges as possible.

    When cool, lift from pans using spatula and break into bite-size pieces.

Praline

Makes about 1¹/₂ cups

¹/₂ cup sugar
3 tablespoons water

Warm Toasted Nuts*

Lightly oil baking sheet. Put sugar in heavy small saucepan and add 3 tablespoons water. Heat over low heat, swirling pan occasionally, until sugar dissolves. Increase heat and boil until mixture begins to brown, brushing down any sugar crystals on sides of pan with wet pastry brush. Continue cooking, swirling pan gently, just until mixture turns rich brown caramel color and trace of smoke begins to rise from pan. Do not allow caramel to get too dark or praline will be bitter; if caramel is too light, praline will be too sweet. Immediately remove from heat and gently add nuts. Stir over low heat until nuts are well coated and caramel thickens slightly, about 1¹/₂ minutes. Immediately pour out onto prepared sheet. Cool completely.

    Break praline into 1-inch pieces. To coarsely chop, transfer to processor and chop using on/off turns. To make praline powder, grind in processor, stopping occasionally to scrape mixture towards center. (*Praline can be stored in airtight container 3 weeks at room temperature or frozen 3 months.*)

Warm Toasted Nuts

For almonds: Preheat oven to 400°F. Toast ³/₄ cup almonds in shallow pan until light brown, about 8 minutes.

For hazelnuts: Preheat oven to 350°F. Toast ³/₄ cup hazelnuts in shallow pan until skins begin to split, about 8 minutes. Transfer to large strainer. Rub nuts against strainer with terrycloth towel to remove most skins.

For pecans or walnuts: Preheat oven to 350°F. Toast 1 cup nuts in shallow baking pan 5 minutes.

Macadamia Nut Fudge

Makes about 128 1-inch squares

4¹/₂ cups sugar (2 pounds)
¹/₂ cup (1 stick) unsalted butter
1 13-ounce can evaporated milk
3 4-ounce bars sweet cooking chocolate (best quality)
1 12-ounce package semisweet chocolate chips
1 7-ounce jar marshmallow cream

1 teaspoon salt
2 teaspoons vanilla
3 cups coarsely chopped unsalted raw macadamia nuts (chop by placing in plastic bag and pounding with mallet or heavy rolling pin)

Line 2 9-inch square pans with waxed paper. Combine sugar, butter and milk in heavy 2-quart saucepan and bring to simmer over medium heat. *At first sign of a bubble, simmer 5 minutes, stirring constantly.* Remove from heat and add all ingredients except 1 cup nuts.

Spread into pans. Sprinkle with remaining nuts, pressing lightly into surface. Chill until firm. Cut into squares.

Chocolate-Covered Brandied Cherries

Start soaking the cherries for this classic candy at least three weeks ahead.

Makes about 36

Cherries
1 pound fresh cherries, pitted (with stems) or one 15-ounce jar cherries in brandy (with stems), drained
Brandy
4 whole cloves
2 2-inch cinnamon sticks

Fondant
1 pound sugar
¹/₂ cup water
¹/₄ cup light corn syrup

8 to 12 ounces semisweet chocolate, grated and tempered (see box, page 109)

For cherries: Marinate fresh or preserved cherries in brandy to cover with cloves and cinnamon at least 3 weeks.

For fondant: Dampen marble or other nonwooden work surface. Line baking sheet with waxed paper. Stir sugar, water and corn syrup in heavy medium saucepan with wooden spoon until sugar dissolves. Place over medium-high heat and bring to boil, without stirring, washing down crystals on sides of pan with wet pastry brush. Let boil until candy thermometer registers 234°F (soft-ball stage). Pour mixture onto dampened surface. Working with dough scraper or metal spatula, lift and fold mixture repeatedly from edges to center until silky and pure white. Fondant will stiffen to point where it no longer can be kneaded.

Transfer fondant to heavy saucepan and warm over low heat, stirring constantly with wooden spoon until just melted; do not overheat. Fondant should be smooth, glossy and coat back of spoon. Remove from heat. Drain cherries and pat dry. Holding cherries by stems, dip into melted fondant until ³/₄ submerged.

Dip back onto surface of fondant (but not quite into it) in sharp up and down motion, letting excess fondant be pulled back into pan. Smooth base of cherries on edge of pan, swirling in clockwise motion. Arrange on prepared sheet. Let stand until set and dry to touch.

Arrange foil candy cups on baking sheet. Holding cherries by stem, dip into tempered chocolate, rotating to cover completely. Cool in dry place 4 days. Store cherries in foil- or waxed paper-lined airtight container for up to 6 weeks.

Chocolate-Coated Cherry Surprises

Makes 25 to 28 candies

¹/₂ cup creamy-style peanut butter
¹/₂ cup powdered sugar, sifted
1 tablespoon unsalted butter, room temperature
2 teaspoons vanilla

25 to 28 maraschino cherries with stems (at least one 8-ounce jar—the count varies), drained

Dipping Chocolate
5 ounces semisweet chocolate
1 tablespoon oil (preferably safflower)

Line baking sheet with waxed paper. Combine first 4 ingredients in small bowl and mix well. Shape into 25 to 28 balls about ³/₄ inch in diameter and set on baking sheet. Chill well.

Pat cherries dry with paper towels. Press peanut butter balls to flatten and carefully wrap around cherries, encasing to base of stem. Return to baking sheet and chill at least 3 hours.

For dipping: Melt chocolate and oil in small saucepan over hot, not boiling, water. *Do not allow any water to drop into chocolate; this would cause it to thicken.* Keep chocolate between 100°F and 110°F on candy thermometer.

Working in cool place (68°F or less), hold each cherry by stem and dip into chocolate (tilt pan to get as much depth as possible); use back of spoon to remove any excess chocolate on base of cherries. Return to baking sheet and refrigerate until firm, at least 2 hours.

Toasted Coconut Marshmallows

These yummy homemade marshmallows are best if eaten within 24 hours.

Makes 70 to 75 1¹/₄-inch squares

1 fresh coconut *or* about 1¹/₂ cups packaged flaked coconut, toasted

2 envelopes unflavored gelatin
³/₄ cup cold water

1¹/₂ cups sugar
¹/₂ cup firmly packed light brown sugar

³/₄ cup boiling water
¹/₈ teaspoon salt

¹/₂ cup whole or halved blanched almonds, lightly toasted and finely ground
1 tablespoon vanilla

If using fresh coconut: Preheat oven to 350°F. Pierce the 3 depressions on top of coconut with ice pick or large nail and hammer; drain out liquid. Set coconut in pan and bake until shell cracks open, about 20 minutes. Wrap in dish towel and hit with hammer to break shell into pieces. Separate meat from shell and remove skin with vegetable peeler. Shred coconut. Spread in shallow pan and bake until browned, stirring twice, about 20 to 25 minutes.

Lightly butter 2 8-inch square pans. Sprinkle gelatin over cold water and let stand until liquid is absorbed.

Combine sugars, water and salt in large heavy saucepan. Place over medium heat and stir only until sugar dissolves. Continue cooking without stirring until syrup reaches 280°F on candy thermometer (soft-crack stage).

Pour into large bowl of electric mixer and add gelatin. Beat at low speed 3 minutes, then at medium speed 10 minutes. Mix in almonds and vanilla.

Spread into buttered pans and refrigerate until firm, about 45 minutes.

To cut, dip metal spatula in hot water, then begin slicing marshmallow into squares, dipping spatula before each cut. Roll squares in coconut. Store in airtight container in cool dark place.

Marzipan Fruit and Animals

Makes about 40 pieces

Marzipan
1 pound almond paste
1 pound powdered sugar
Kirsch

Peaches
Orange, red and green food coloring
Whole cloves

Pears
Yellow, green and red food coloring
Whole cloves

Mice
Halved almonds
Melted chocolate

For marzipan: Knead almond paste, sugar and enough kirsch to make mixture pliable (consistency of soft clay).

For peaches: Work orange food coloring into 1/3 of marzipan (wrap remainder in plastic to prevent drying). Roll into about 16 balls, slightly longer than wide. Make characteristic peach indentation from top to bottom with dull edge of knife. Press clove in top for stem. Paint shadings of peach onto marzipan using soft brush dipped in diluted red and green food coloring.

For pears: Work yellow and green food coloring into 1/3 of marzipan (wrap remainder in plastic to prevent drying). Roll into about 15 cylinders. Applying pressure on one side only, roll back and forth to achieve pear shape. Round both ends with fingers. Press whole clove in top for stem and star end of clove in bottom. Paint blush of pear onto marzipan using soft brush dipped in diluted red food coloring.

For mice: Roll most of remaining marzipan into 8 rounds the size of golf balls, reserving remainder for "tails." Roll ball into fat cylinder. Applying more pressure on one end, roll to achieve cone shape with rounded ends. Roll remaining marzipan into very thin 2½-inch "tails" and attach to cones with water. For ears, stand halved almonds in "head," flat sides forward. Fill paper cone with melted chocolate and pipe on eyes and whiskers. Store in foil-lined airtight container in cool dry place up to 6 weeks.

Variations

To create other shapes:

For bananas—Tint marzipan yellow. Roll into 3-inch lengths, tapering ends. Paint with melted semisweet chocolate.

For oranges—Tint marzipan orange. Shape into 1½-inch rounds. Texture by gently rolling on fine mesh grater. Tint additional marzipan green for stems.

For pigs—Tint marzipan pink. Shape golf ball-size piece into fat cylinder. Pull legs on "bottom" side. Choose one end for front and make round or pointed head, then push in to blunt nose. Use additional marzipan to shape ears and curly tail. Pipe dots of melted chocolate for eyes.

❦ Index

Almond(s)
Bark, 104
Bundkuchen, 79
-Cheese Diamonds, 66
Garlic, 5
Praline, 111
-Walnut Butter Toffee, 102
Alsatian Cheese Spread, 2
Anadama Rolls with
Orange Butter, 68
Anchoiade (Tapénade), 2
Appetizer. See also Pâté; Relish;
Terrine
Anchoiade, 2
Eggplant Laura, 42
Peppers, Turkish Stuffed, 44
Mushrooms, Marinated, 38
Potato Caponata, 42
Apple
Apricot and Walnut Chutney, 46
-Cardamom Butter, 59
Catsup, Spicy, 48
and Currant Strudel, 73
Dried, and Molasses Cake, 82
-Loquat Preserves, 56
Pepper Jelly, 52
Syrup, Spicy, 23
and Veal Terrine with Green
Peppercorns and Calvados, 13
Applesauce, Gin and
Juniper-Spiced, 23
Apricot(s)
Apple and Walnut Chutney, 46
Cake, Easy, 83
-Macadamia Nut Fruitcake, 88
Orange Braid, 76
Preserves, Chunky, 56
in Rum with Ginger and
Sultanas, 60
Sauce, 23

Bachelor's Confiture (Fruit Soaked in
Vodka), 59

Banana-Macadamia Nut Bread, 70
Banana Yeast Bread, 70
Barbecue Sauce and Marinade, 22
Basil Vinegar, Fresh, 26
Beef and Veal Terrine with Whole
Mushrooms, 12
Beet Preserves, Viennese, 56
Bittersweet Chocolate Caramels with
Burnt Almonds, 103
Black Pepper Sauce, 19
Blue Cheese, Maytag, Shortbread, 66
Blueberry-Mint Vinegar, 28
Brandy(ied)
Cherries, 61
Cherries, Chocolate-covered, 112
Peaches in, 61
Pineapple in, 62
Prunes, 62
Vanilla Essence, 25
Bread. See also Shortbread; Sweet
Bread
Banana Yeast, 70
Challah, Minnie's, 68
Country, Della Robbia Loaf, 67
Ginger Breadmen, Jumbo, 81
Sticks, Rosemary-Dill, 65
Sticks, Sage Cheddar, 65
Breakfast Pies, Roast Pork and
Apple, 10
Brittle, Peanut, Old-Fashioned, 111
Brittle, Sunflower Seed, 111
Brownies
Brown Sugar Pecan, 98
Double Fudge Muffins, 80
Rococo's, 98
Toffee Fudge, 97
Burgundy Wine and Honey Sauce, 25
Butter. See Fruit Butter

Cake. See also Fruitcake; Sweet
Breads
Almond Bundkuchen, 79
Apple, Dried, and Molassess, 82

Apricot, Easy, 83
Cheesecake with
Streusel Topping, 79
Cinnamon Nut Wreath, 74
Coffee, Grossmutti's, 78
Coffee, Orange Apricot Braid, 76
Date, 90
Gateau Breton, 86
Gingerbread, Grandmother's, 83
Gingerbread House,
Old-Fashioned, 92
Honey, 84
Pound, Fudge Chip, 87
Pound, Old World Sour Cream, 82
Rum-Raisin Kugelhopf, 75
Sesame Streusel, 84
Stollen, Ground Nut, German
Goese, 77
Strudel Apple and Currant, 73
Candy. See Confection
Caponata, Potato, 42
Caramel(s)
Bittersweet Chocolate with Burnt
Almonds, 103
Creamy, 101
Moux (Candy), 100
Sauce, Southwest, 24
Caramelized Orange Sections, 100
Cashew Nuts, Peppery Indian, 3
Catsup, Spicy Apple, 48
Castup, Walnut-Plum, 49
Celery Flavored Dijon Mustard, 31
Certosino (Bolognese Fruitcake), 92
Challah, Minnie's, 68
Cheese
-Almond Diamonds, 66
Cheddar Sage Breadsticks, 65
-Garlic Popcorn, 5
Hickory-smoked Cheddar
Crackers, 64
Shortbread, Maytag Blue, 66
Spread, Alsatian, 2
Spread, Cumin, 2

Cheese (continued)
 Spread, Viennese Liptauer, 2
 Wafers, LBJ Ranch, 64
Cheesecake with Streusel Topping
 (Kasekuchen), 79
Cherry(ies)
 Brandied, 61
 Brandied, Chocolate-covered, 112
 Surprises, Chocolate-coated, 113
Chili. See also Green Chili Roasted
 Peanuts, 3
 Sauce, 20
Chilies, Pickled Pepper Sauce, 19
Chinese-Style Sun-Dried
 Tomatoes, 43
Chocolate
 About Tempering, 109
 Caramels, Bittersweet, with Burnt
  Almonds, 103
 Chip Fudge Pound Cake, 87
 Chip Mocha Cookies, 95
 Chip Walnut Praline Cookies, 96
 -coated Cherry Surprises, 113
 Confection with Raspberries, 107
 -covered Brandied Cherries, 112
 Cranberry Truffles, 109
 Cutouts (Candy), 102
 Double Fudge Muffins, 80
 Peanut Butter Balls, 106
 Peanut Clusters, 103
 Sauce, Hot Fudge, 24
 Truffles, Grand Marnier, 108
Chorizo, Smoked, 8
Christmas. See Holiday
Christmas Fruitcake Soufflé, 86
Chutney
 Apple, Apricot and Walnut, 46
 Cranberry, 46
 Lemon-Fig, 47
 Mango, Quick, 47
 Pineapple-Papaya, 48
 Tomato Macadamia Nut, 46
Cilantro Pesto, 18
Cinnamon Nut Wreath, 74
Citrus Marmalade, Amber Clove, 54
Coconut
 Granola, 6
 Honey Loaf, 72
 Marshmallows, Toasted, 113
 Snowballs, 108
Coffee Cake. See Cake
Compote, Spiked Fruit, 60
Condiments. See Chutney;
 Jam; Sauce
Confection
 Almond Bark, 104
 Brandied Cherries, Chocolate-
  covered, 112
 Caramel Moux, 100
 Caramels, Bittersweet Chocolate
  with Burnt Almonds, 103
 Caramels, Creamy, 101
 Cherry Surprises, Chocolate-
  coated, 113

Chocolate Cutouts, 102
Chocolate Peanut Butter Balls, 106
Chocolate Peanut Clusters, 103
Chocolate with Raspberries, 107
Coconut Marshmallows,
 Toasted, 113
Coconut Snowballs, 108
Date and Peanut Butter Balls, 107
Fruit and Nut Rolls, 100
Fudge, Macadamia Nut, 112
Gianduja "Bacon," 105
Marzipan Fruit and Animals, 114
Nougat Dish, 104
Nougat Montelimar, 104
Nutmegs, 101
Orange Sections, Caramelized, 100
Peanut Brittle, Old-Fashioned, 111
Peanut Butter Feuilleté, 106
Praline, 111
Rocky Road, 103
Sunflower Seed Brittle, 111
Toffee, Almond-Walnut Butter, 102
Toffee, English Butter, 105
Truffles, Chocolate Cranberry, 109
Truffles, Grand Marnier
 Chocolate, 108
Truffles, Mint, 110
Confiture, Bachelor's, 59
Conserve. See Relish
Cookies. See also Brownies
 Lebkuchen Bars with Lemon
  Glaze, Nürnberger, 96
 Maple Syrup Shortbreads, 95
 Mocha Chocolate Chip, 95
 Sweet Semolina Diamonds, 94
 Walnut Praline Chocolate Chip, 96
 Windmill, 95
Crackers
 Blue Cheese Shortbread,
  Maytag, 66
 Cheese-Almond Diamonds, 66
 Hickory-smoked Cheddar, 64
 Indian (Matthi), 64
 LBJ Ranch Cheese Wafers, 64
Cranberry
 Cassis Preserves, 56
 Chocolate Truffles, 109
 Chutney, 46
 -Grapefruit Marmalade,
  Gingered, 55
 Vinegar, 28
Cumberland Sauce, 20
Cumin Cheese Spread, 2
Currant and Apple Strudel, 73
Curry Paste, 36

Date Cake, 90
Date and Peanut Butter Balls, 107
Della Robbia Loaf, 67
Dessert. See Cake; Cookies; etc.
Dessert Sauce
 Apple Syrup, Spicy, 23
 Apricot, 23
 Brandied Vanilla Essence, 25

Caramel, Southwest, 24
Gin and Juniper-Spiced
 Applesauce, 23
Grandmother's, 25
Hot Fudge, 24
Kumquat, Japanese, 22
Pineapple, Spiked, 24
Dijon Mayonnaise, 20
Dijon Mustard Vinaigrette, 29
Dijon Mustards, Flavored, 30 – 31
Dresden Stollen, 77
Dressing. See also Sauce
 Mayonnaise, Dijon, 20
 Onion Salad, 30
 Polli's House, 30
 Poppy Seed, 30
 Vinaigrette, Dijon Mustard, 29

Easter Bread, Sweet, 73
Eggplant Laura, 42
Eggs, English Pub-Style Pickled, 41
Eggs, Pickled Ruby, 41
English
 Butter Toffee, 105
 Guinness Fruitcake, 89
 Plum Pudding, 85
 Pub Mustard, 34
 Pub-Style Pickled Eggs, 41

Fig-Lemon Chutney, 47
Five-Day Pickles, 38
Flavored Mustard(s)
 About Making to Give, 33
 Dijon, 30 – 31
 English Pub, 34
 Green Chili with Green
  Peppercorns, 32
 Monk-Style Black
  Mustard Seed, 34
 Red Pepper, Roasted, 32
 Spicy Molasses, 33
Flavored Oil(s)
 Herb-infused, Fresh, 29
 Olive, Double, 29
 Olive, with Porcini Mushrooms,
  Garlic and Herbs, 29
 Sun-Dried Italian Tomatoes in, 43
Flavored Vinegar
 Basil, Fresh, 26
 Cranberry, 28
 Fruit, Basic, 27; variations, 28
 Ginger and Spice, 28
 Herb, Basic, 26
 Peppered Old South, Hot, 27
 Rose Petal, 28
 Rosemary or Thyme, 27
The Four Seasons Fruitcake, 91
French Country Pâté de Campagne, 14
Fruit. See also Jam; Marmalade;
 Name of Fruit; Preserves
 Compote, Spiked, 60
 and Nut Rolls, 100
 Soaked in vodka (Bachelor's
  Confiture), 59

and Vegetable Muffins, Golden, 80
Vinegar, Basic, 27
Fruit Butter
Apple-Cardamom, 59
Orange, 69
Pear Vanilla, 58
Prune-Port, 58
Fruit in Liqueur
Apricots in Rum with Ginger and
Sultanas, 60
Cherries, Brandied, 61
Peaches in Brandy, 61
Pineapple in Brandy, 62
Plums, Spiced Damson, 62
Poire (Pear), Eau de Vie de, 61
Prunes, Brandied, 62
Fruitcake
Apricot-Macadamia Nut, 88
Certosino (from Bologna), 92
The Four Seasons, 91
Guinness English, 89
Mother's, 90
Scotch Bun, 88
Soufflé, Christmas, 86
Fudge
Chip Pound Cake, 87
Macadamia Nut, 112
Muffins, Double, 80
Toffee Brownies, 97

Garam Masala, 34
Garlic Almonds, 5
Gateau Breton, 86
Genoese Red Pesto, 18
German Goese Ground Nut
Stollen, 77
Gianduja "Bacon" (Candy), 105
Giardiniera (Italian Pickled
Vegetables), 40
Gin and Juniper-Spiced
Applesauce, 23
Ginger Breadman, Jumbo, 81
Ginger and Spice Vinegar, 28
Gingerbread, Grandmother's, 83
Gingerbread House,
Old-Fashioned, 92
Gingered Cranberry-Grapefruit
Marmalade, 55
Glazed Pecans, 4
Glazed Spiced Nuts, 4
Grand Marnier Chocolate
Truffles, 108
Grandmother's Gingerbread, 83
Grandmother's Sauce, 25
Granola, Coconut, 6
Grapefruit-Cranberry Marmalade,
Gingered, 55
Greek Lemon-Fig Chutney, 47
Greek Olives, Marinated, 45
Green Chili Condiment, New
Mexico, 43
Green Chili Mustard with Green
Peppercorns, 32
Green Peppers. See Peppers

Green Sauce, 18
Grossmutti's Coffee Cake, 78
Guinness English Fruitcake, 89

Hard Sauce, 86
Herb-infused Oil, Fresh, 29
Herb Vinegar, Basic, 26
Herbed
Breadsticks, Rosemary-Dill, 65
Pear Jam, 52
Sausage, 9
Seasoning, 35
Veal and Pork Pâté with
Pistachios, 12
Herbes de Provence Flavored Dijon
Mustard, 30
Hickory-smoked Cheddar
Crackers, 64
Holiday Foods
Bread, Dresden Stollen, 77
Bread, Ginger Breadmen,
Jumbo, 81
Bread, Serpentona, 71
Cookies, Nürnberger Lebkuchen
with Lemon Glaze, 96
Dessert, Plum Puddings, 85
Fruitcake, Guinness English, 89
Fruitcake Soufflé, Christmas, 86
Mints, Deluxe, 102
Sweet Bread, Easter, 73
Wreath, Della Robbia Loaf, 67
Honey Cake, 84
Honey Coconut Loaf, 72
Honeyed Walnuts, 4
Hot Fudge Sauce, 24

Indian Crackers (Matthi), 64
Italian Pickled Vegetables
(Giardiniera), 40
Italian Tomatoes, Sun-Dried in
Flavored Oils, 43

Jam and Jelly. See also Marmalade;
Preserves
Apple Pepper, 52
Herbed Pear, 52
Red Pepper, 52
Japanese Kumquat Sauce, 22
Jerusalem Artichoke Relish, 43

Kosher Pickles, 38
Kugelhopf, Rum-Raisin, 75
Kumquat Sauce, Japanese, 22

LBJ Ranch Cheese Wafers, 64
Lebkuchen Bars with Lemon Glaze,
Nürnberger, 96
Lemon
-Fig Chutney, 47
Flavored (au Citron) Dijon
Mustard, 31
-Mustard Sauce, 19
Poppy Seed Bread, Penelope's, 72
Lime Flavored Dijon Mustard, 31
Loquat-Apple Preserves, 56

Macadamia Nut
Apricot Fruitcake, 88
Banana Bread, 70
Fudge, 112
Tomato Chutney, 46
Mango Chutney, Quick, 47
Maple Syrup Shortbreads, 95
Marinade and Barbecue Sauce, 22
Marinated Greek Olives, 45
Marinated Mushrooms,
Mediterranean-Style, 38
Marmalade
Citrus, Amber Clove, 54
Five-Fruit, 54
Gingered Cranberry-Grapefruit, 55
(Orange) Marvelous Microwave, 53
Red Onion and Rosemary with
Cassis, 53
Marshmallows, Coconut,
Toasted, 113
Marzipan, 91
Marzipan Fruit and Animals, 114
Mayonnaise, Dijon, 20
Mediterranean-Style Marinated
Mushrooms, 38
Microwave Marmalade (Orange),
Marvelous, 53
Mincemeat, 50
Mincemeat, Walnut and Pear,
Double, 49
Minnie's Challah, 68
Mint Truffles, 110
Mints, Deluxe Holiday, 102
Mocha Chocolate Chip Cookies, 95
Molasses and Dried Apple Cake, 82
Molasses Mustard, Spicy, 33
Monk-Style Black Mustard Seed
Mustard, 34
Mother's Fruitcake, 90
Muffins, Double Fudge, 80
Muffins, Fruit and Vegetable,
Golden, 80
Mushrooms, Marinated,
Mediterranean-Style, 38
Mushrooms, Porcini, Garlic and
Herbs, Olive Oil Flavored with, 29
Mustard. See also Flavored Mustard
Dijon, Vinaigrette, 29
-Lemon Sauce, 19
Sauce, Cold, 19
-Sesame Sauce, 20

Nougat Candy Dish, 104
Nougat Montelimar, 104
Nut(s). See also Name of Nut
Cinnamon Wreath, 74
and Fruit Rolls, 100
Glazed Spiced, 4
Stollen, German Goese
Ground, 77
Nutmegs, 101

Oil. See Flavored Oil
Olive Oil, Double, 29

Olive Oil Flavored with Porcini
  Mushrooms, Garlic and Herbs, 29
Olives
  Marinated Greek, 45
  Noires, Flavored Dijon Mustard, 31
  Piquant, 45
Onion(s)
  Pickled, 39
  Red, and Rosemary Marmalade
    with cassis, 53
  Salad Dressing, 30
Orange
  Apricot Braid, 76
  Butter, 69
  Marmalade, Marvelous
    Microwave, 53
  Sections, Caramelized, 100

Papaya-Pinapple Chutney, 48
Pâté. See also Terrine
  de Campagne, 14
  Herbed Veal and Pork, with
    Pistachios, 12
  Spinach, 11
Peach-Ginger Vinegar, 28
Peaches in Brandy, 61
Peanut(s)
  Brittle, Old-Fashioned, 111
  Butter Chocolate Balls, 106
  Butter and Date Balls, 107
  Butter Feuilleté (Candy), 106
  Chili Roasted, 3
  Chocolate Clusters, 103
Pear
  Eau de Vie de Poire, 61
  Jam, Herbed, 52
  Vanilla Butter, 58
  and Walnut Mincemeat,
    Double, 49
Pecan(s)
  Brown Sugar Brownies, 98
  Glazed, 4
  Spiced, 3
Pepper(s). See also Red Pepper
  Apple Jelly, 52
  Black, Sauce, 19
  Pickled (Chilies) Sauce, 19
  Preserved in Vinegar (Peperoni
    Sott' Aceto), 39
  Turkish Stuffed, 44
Peppered Old South Vinegar, Hot, 27
Peppery Indian Cashew Nuts (Bhone
  Kaaju), 3
Pesto, Cilantro, 18
Pesto, Genoese Red, 18
Pickled
  Eggs, English Pub-Style, 41
  Eggs, Ruby, 41
  Onions, 39
  Pepper Sauce, 19
  Peppers Preserved in Vinegar, 39
  Plums in Vinegar,
    Chef Gaertner's, 39

Vegetables, Italian, 40
Pickles. See also Relishes
  Five-Day, 38
  Kosher, 38
  Squash, Sweet Yellow, 40
Pies, Breakfast, Roast Pork and
  Apple, 10
Pineapple
  in Brandy, 62
  Dessert Sauce, Spiked, 24
  -Papaya Chutney, 48
Piquant Olives, 45
Plum(s)
  Pudding, 85; English, 85
  Spiced Damson, 62
  in Vinegar, Chef Gaertner's, 39
  Walnut Catsup, 49
Polli's House Dressing, 30
Popcorn, Cheese-Garlic, 5
Poppy Seed Dressing, 30
Poppy Seed Lemon Bread,
  Penelope's, 72
Porcini Mushrooms, Garlic and
  Herbs, Olive Oil Flavored with, 29
Pork Roast and Apple Breakfast
  Pies, 10
Pork and Veal Pâté, Herbed with
  Pistachios, 12
Potato Caponata, 42
Pound Cake, Fudge Chip, 87
Pound Cake, Old World
  Sour Cream, 82
Praline, 111
Preserves. See also Jam; Marmalade
  About Making Perfect, 57
  Apricot, Chunky, 56
  Beet, Viennese, 56
  Cranberry Cassis, 56
  Loquat-Apple, 56
Prune(s)
  Brandied, 62
  Cake, Gateau Breton, 86
  -Port Butter, 58
Pudding, Plum, 85; English, 85
Pumpkin Loaf, Spiced, 69

Rabbit, Terrine of, 16
Raisin-Rum Kugelhopf, 75
Rancho Mole Sauce, 21
Raspberries, Chocolate Confection
  with, 107
Red Onion and Rosemary
  Marmalade with Cassis, 53
Red Pepper
  Jelly, 52
  Mustard, Roasted, 32
  Relish, 44
Relish. See also Appetizer; Chutney;
  Pickles
  Jerusalem Artichoke, 43
  Olives, Marinated Greek, 45
  Olives, Piquant, 45
  Red Pepper, 44

Tomato Conserve, 48
Rocky Road (Candy), 103
Rococo's Brownies, 98
Rolls, Anadama with
  Orange Butter, 69
Rose Petal Vinegar, 28
Rosemary
  -Dill Bread Sticks, 65
  Roasted Walnuts, 5
  or Thyme Vinegar, 27
Rum-Raisin Kugelhopf, 75

Sage Cheddar Breadsticks, 65
Salad Dressing. See Dressing
Salt, Seasoning, 9
Sauce. See also Dessert Sauce
  Barbecue, and Marinade, 22
  Black Pepper, 19
  Burgundy Wine and Honey, 25
  Catsup, Spicy Apple, 48
  Catsup, Walnut-Plum, 49
  Chili, 20
  Cumberland, 20
  Green, 18
  Green Chili, Condiment, 43
  Hard, 86
  Lemon-Mustard, 19
  Mustard, Cold, 19
  Pesto, Cilantro, 18
  Pesto, Genoese Red, 18
  Pickled Pepper, 19
  Rancho Mole, 21
  Sesame-Mustard, 20
  Tomato, Chunky, 22
  Tomato, Quick, 42
Sausage(s)
  Chorizo, Smoked, 8
  Herbed, 9
  Homemade Red Wine, 8
Scotch Bun, 88
Seasoning Salt, 9
Seasonings
  Curry Paste, 36
  Garam Masala, 34
  Herbed, 35
  Sonoran, 35
  Spicy Blend, 35
  Terrine Spice Mixture, 15
Semolina Diamonds, Sweet, 94
Serpentona (Holiday Bread), 71
Sesame-Mustard Sauce, 20
Sesame Streusel Cake, 84
Shallot Flavored Dijon Mustard (aux
  Echalotes), 31
Shortbread. See Crackers
Shortbreads, Maple Syrup, 95
Sonoran Seasoning, 35
Soufflé, Christmas Fruitcake, 86
Sour Cream Pound Cake, Old World, 82
Southwest Caramel Sauce, 24
Spice Mixture for Terrine, 15
Spiced
  Damson Plums, 62

Pecans, 3
Pumpkin Loaf, 69
Spicy
    Apple Catsup, 48
    Apple Syrup, 23
    Blend, Seasoning, 35
    Molasses Mustard, 33
Spiked Fruit Compote, 60
Spiked Pineapple Dessert Sauce, 24
Spinach Pâté, 11
Spread. See Cheese Spread
Squash Pickles, Sweet Yellow, 40
Stollen, Dresden, 77
Stollen, Ground Nut, German
    Goese, 77
Strudel Apple and Currant, 73
Sun-Dried Italian Tomatoes in
    Flavored Oils, 43
Sunflower Seed Brittle, 111
Sweet Bread. See also Bread; Cake
    Banana-Macadamia Nut, 70
    Dresden Stollen, 77
    Easter, 73
    Honey Coconut Loaf, 72
    Lemon Poppy Seed, Penelope's, 72
    Pumpkin Loaf, Spiced, 69
    Serpentona, 71
    Walnut, 72

Sweet Sauce. See Dessert Sauce

Tapénade (Anchoiade), 2
Terrine. See also Pâté
    of Beef and Veal with Whole
        Mushrooms, 12
    à l'Orange, 14
    of Rabbit, 16
    Veal and Apple with Green
        Peppercorns and Calvados, 13
Thyme or Rosemary Vinegar, 27
Toffee
    Almond-Walnut Butter, 102
    English Butter, 105
    Fudge Brownies, 97
Tomato(es)
    Conserve, 48
    Macadamia Nut Chutney, 46
    Sauce, Chunky, 22
    Sauce, Quick, 42
    Sun-Dried Italian in Flavored
        Oils, 43;
        variations, 43
Truffles
    Chocolate Cranberry, 109
    Chocolate, Grand Marnier, 108
    Mint, 110
Turkish Stuffed Peppers, 44

Veal
    and Apple Terrine with Green
        Peppercorns and Calvados, 13
    and Beef Terrine with Whole
        Mushrooms, 12
    and Pork Pâté, Herbed with
        Pistachios, 12
Vegetable and Fruit Muffins, 80
Vegetables, Italian Pickled, 40
Viennese Beet Preserves, 56
Viennese Liptauer, 2
Vinaigrette, Dijon Mustard, 29
Vinegar. See also Flavored Vinegar
    Peppers Preserved in, 39
    Plums in, Chef Gaertner's, 39

Walnut(s)
    and Apple Chutney, 46
    Bread, 72
    Honeyed, 4
    and Pear Mincemeat, Double, 49
    -Plum Catsup, 49
    Praline, 111
    Praline Chocolate Chip
        Cookies, 96
    Rosemary Roasted, 5
Windmill Cookies, 95
Wine, Burgundy, and Honey Sauce, 25

Credits and Acknowledgments

The following people contributed the recipes included in this book:

Jean Anderson
Elizabeth Andoh
John and Demetra Andronico
Paola Bagnatori
Nancy Barr
Joan and Wade Baxley
James Beard
Paul Bhalla
Margaret Biles
Donna Blatherwick
Mary Lou Bone
Jean Brady
Mary Bryant
Betty Budlong
Bobby and Laura Cadwallader
Biba Caggiano
Lois Carita
Irene Chalmers
John Chesteen
Lily Chu
Shirley Collins
Cranberry Moose, Yarmouthport,
    Massachusetts
Pat Connell
Kerri Culbertson
Mary Dame
Jamie Davies
Dierdre Davis
Connie De Brenes
Joe Famularo
Dee Fleming
The Four Seasons, New York City,
    New York
Yvonne Gill
Gerri Gilliland
Connie Glenn
Julie Gordon
Marion Gorman

Grand Central Oyster Bar, New York
    City, New York
Bert Greene
Anne Lindsay Greer
Zack Hanle
Barbara Hansen
Marie Hasman
Ruedi Hauser
The Hay-Adams, Washington, D.C.
Lyn Heller
Christopher Horan
Susan Horn
John Hurst
Izaak Walton Inn, Glacier National Park,
    Montana
Sally Jordan
Jane Helsel Joseph
Lynne Kasper
Bob Kasser
Vince and Ouida Kelly
Kristine Kidd
Jean Kressy
Loni Kuhn
Louise Lamensdorf
Faye Levy
Darlene Lieblich
Mimmetta Lo Monte
Susan Herrman Loomis
Abby Mandel
Mary Manilla
Linda Marino
Michael McLaughlin
Jacqueline McMahan
Roberta Meshel
Barbara Miachika
Jefferson and Jinx Morgan
Nevele Country Club, Ellenville, New Jersey
Donna Nordin

Beatrice Ojakangas
Old Apple Farm, Kansas City, Missouri
Penelope's Restaurant, Crested Butte,
    Colorado
Sara Perry
Polli's On The Beach, Kihei, Maui
Thelma Pressman
Michele Roberts
Rococo Chocolates, Portland, Oregon
Franco and Margaret Romagnoli
Ronnie's, Orlando, Florida
Betty Rosbottom
Julie Sahni
Ailene Sarappo
Arno Schmidt
Sylvia Schur
Patricia Schwartz
Edena Sheldon
Nettie Smothers
Some Crust Bakery, Claremont, California
Bonnie Stern
Renie Steves
The Tangaroa Terrace, Walt Disney World,
    Florida
Dorothea Taylor
Jane Trittipo
Susann Turok
Maggie Waldron
Jack Webster
Jan Weimer
Alice Welsh
Anne Willan
Alan Zeman
Gilda Zimmar
Additional text was supplied by:
Ruedi Hauser, *Chocolate Tempering Tips;*
    Loni Kuhn, *Perfect Preserves;* Edena
    Sheldon, *Making Mustards to Give.*

Special thanks to:

Editorial Staff:
    Angeline Vogl
    Mary Jane Bescoby

Graphics Staff:
    Bernard Rotondo
    Gloriane Harris

Rights and Permissions:
    Karen Legier

Indexer:
    Rose Grant

The Knapp Press
is a wholly owned subsidiary of
Knapp Communications Corporation.

Composition by Andresen Typographics, Tucson

This book is set in Sabon, a face designed by Jan Teischold in 1967
and based on early fonts engraved by Garamond and Granjon.